Cambridge English

FIRST for Schools 1

FIRST CERTIFICATE IN ENGLISH FOR SCHOOLS

WITHOUT ANSWERS

AUTHENTIC EXAMINATION PAPERS
FROM CAMBRIDGE ENGLISH
LANGUAGE ASSESSMENT

For revised exam from 2015

Cambridge University Press
www.cambridge.org/elt

Cambridge Assessment English
www.cambridgeenglish.org

Information on this title: www.cambridge.org/9781107692671

© Cambridge University Press and UCLES 2014

It is normally necessary for written permission for copying to be obtained *in advance* from a publisher. The sample answer sheets at the back of this book are designed to be copied and distributed in class.
The normal requirements are waived here and it is not necessary to write to Cambridge University Press for permission for an individual teacher to make copies for use within his or her own classroom. Only those pages that carry the wording '© UCLES 2014 Photocopiable' may be copied.

First published 2014

20 19

Printed in Great Britain by CPI Group (UK) Ltd, Croydon CR0 4YY

A catalogue record for this book is available from the British Library

ISBN 978-1-107-64703-9 Student's Book with answers
ISBN 978-1-107-69267-1 Student's Book without answers
ISBN 978-1-107-66907-9 Audio CDs (2)
ISBN 978-1-107-67209-3 Student's Book Pack (Student's Book with answers and Audio CDs (2))

The publishers have no responsibility for the persistence or accuracy of URLs for external or third-party internet websites referred to in this publication, and do not guarantee that any content on such websites is, or will remain, accurate or appropriate. Information regarding prices, travel timetables, and other factual information given in this work is correct at the time of first printing but the publishers do not guarantee the accuracy of such information thereafter.

Contents

	Introduction	*4*
Test 1	Reading and Use of English	*8*
	Writing	*20*
	Listening	*22*
	Speaking	*28*
Test 2	Reading and Use of English	*30*
	Writing	*42*
	Listening	*44*
	Speaking	*50*
Test 3	Reading and Use of English	*52*
	Writing	*64*
	Listening	*66*
	Speaking	*72*
Test 4	Reading and Use of English	*74*
	Writing	*86*
	Listening	*88*
	Speaking	*94*
	Sample answer sheets	*95*
	Thanks and acknowledgements	*104*
	Visual materials for the Speaking test	*colour section*

Introduction

This collection of four complete practice tests comprises papers from the *Cambridge English: First for Schools* examination; students can practise these tests on their own or with the help of a teacher.

The *Cambridge English: First for Schools* examination is part of a suite of general English examinations produced by Cambridge English Language Assessment. This suite consists of five examinations that have similar characteristics but are designed for different levels of English language ability. Within the five levels, *Cambridge English: First for Schools* is at Level B2 in the Council of Europe's *Common European Framework of Reference for Languages: Learning, teaching, assessment*. It has been accredited by Ofqual, the statutory regulatory authority in England, at Level 1 in the National Qualifications Framework. *The Cambridge English: First for Schools* examination is widely recognised in commerce and industry and in individual university faculties and other educational institutions.

Examination	Council of Europe Framework Level	UK National Qualifications Framework Level
Cambridge English: Proficiency *Certificate of Proficiency in English (CPE)*	C2	3
Cambridge English: Advanced *Certificate in Advanced English (CAE)*	C1	2
Cambridge English: First for Schools *First Certificate in English (FCE) for Schools*	B2	1
Cambridge English: Preliminary *Preliminary English Test (PET)*	B1	Entry 3
Cambridge English: Key *Key English Test (KET)*	A2	Entry 2

Cambridge English: First for Schools follows the same format as *Cambridge English: First* and the level of the question papers is identical. The only difference is that the content and treatment of topics in *Cambridge English: First for Schools* have been particularly targeted at the interest and experience of school pupils. *Cambridge English: First for Schools* candidates who achieve Grade C or higher in the exam, receive a *Cambridge English: First for Schools* certificate.

Further information

The information contained in this practice book is designed to be an overview of the exam. For a full description of all of the above exams, including information about task types, testing focus and preparation, please see the relevant handbooks which can be obtained from Cambridge English Language Assessment at the address below or from the website at: www.cambridgeenglish.org

Cambridge English Language Assessment
1 Hills Road
Cambridge CB1 2EU
United Kingdom

Telephone: +44 1223 553997
Fax: +44 1223 553621
Email: helpdesk@cambridgeenglish.org

The structure of *Cambridge English: First for Schools*: an overview

The *Cambridge English: First for Schools* examination consists of four papers.

Reading and Use of English   1 hour 15 minutes
This paper consists of **seven parts**, with 52 questions. For Parts 1 to 4, the test contains texts with accompanying grammar and vocabulary tasks, and separate items with a grammar and vocabulary focus. For Parts 5 to 7, the test contains a range of texts and accompanying reading comprehension tasks.

Writing   1 hour 20 minutes
This paper consists of **two parts** which carry equal marks. In Part 1, which is **compulsory**, candidates have to write an essay of between 140 and 190 words, giving their opinion in response to a task. In Part 2, there are four tasks from which candidates **choose one** to write about. The range of tasks from which questions may be drawn includes an article, an email/letter, an essay, a review and a short story. The last question is based on a set text. In this part, candidates have to write between 140 and 190 words.

Listening   40 minutes (approximately)
This paper consists of **four parts**. Each part contains a recorded text or texts and some questions, including multiple-choice, sentence completion and multiple-matching. Each text is heard twice. There is a total of **30 questions**.

Speaking   14 minutes
The Speaking test consists of **four parts**. The standard test format is two candidates and two examiners. One examiner takes part in the conversation while the other examiner listens. Both examiners give marks. Candidates will be given photographs and other visual and written materials to look at and talk about. Sometimes candidates will talk with the other candidate, sometimes with the examiner, and sometimes with both.

Introduction

Grading

Candidates will receive a score on the Cambridge English Scale for each of the four skills and Use of English. The average of these five scores gives the candidate's overall Cambridge English Scale score for the exam. This determines what grade and CEFR level they achieve. All candidates receive a Statement of Results and candidates who pass the examination with grade A, B or C also receive the First Certificate in English. Candidates who achieve grade A receive the *First Certificate in English* stating that they demonstrated ability at Level C1. Candidates who achieve grade B or C receive the *First Certificate in English* stating that they demonstrated ability at Level B2. Candidates whose performance is below B2 level, but falls within Level B1, receive a *Cambridge English* certificate stating that they have demonstrated ability at Level B1. Candidates whose performance falls below Level B1 do not receive a certificate.

For further information on grading and results, go to the website (see page 5).

Test 1

Test 1

READING AND USE OF ENGLISH (1 hour 15 minutes)

Part 1

For questions **1–8**, read the text below and decide which answer (**A, B, C** or **D**) best fits each gap. There is an example at the beginning (0).

Mark your answers **on the separate answer sheet**.

Example:

0 A effects   **B** tricks   **C** skills   **D** talents

| 0 | A | **B** | C | D |

BMX racing

Somewhere in California during the early 1970s, a bunch of kids customised their bicycles so they could do **(0)** …….. on them. They were able to do incredibly **(1)** …….. things like jumping off ramps and making their bikes fly through the air. Then they began racing them along dirt tracks. The kids were recorded on camera and the **(2)** …….. film, which was called *On Any Sunday*, **(3)** …….. the word about the new pastime like wildfire. And so a sport **(4)** …….. by kids for kids was born. Bicycle Motocross was the name given to it, which was soon shortened to BMX. It **(5)** …….. the attention of thousands of kids over one short summer.

Nowadays, BMX racing is recognised as a fun action sport. BMX caters for the individual. Every rider gets to take **(6)** …….. . No one sits on the bench and no one ever gets **(7)** …….. from the team. And statistics have proved that, due to the **(8)** …….. safety requirements, it is one of the safest of all youth sports. Have you ever thought of giving BMX a try?

1	**A**	exceptional	**B**	impossible	**C**	excellent	**D**	impressive
2	**A**	resulting	**B**	following	**C**	concluding	**D**	developing
3	**A**	broadened	**B**	extended	**C**	spread	**D**	passed
4	**A**	composed	**B**	created	**C**	formed	**D**	set
5	**A**	took	**B**	earned	**C**	paid	**D**	caught
6	**A**	place	**B**	part	**C**	position	**D**	play
7	**A**	sent	**B**	left	**C**	dropped	**D**	thrown
8	**A**	harsh	**B**	strict	**C**	firm	**D**	strong

Part 2

For questions **9–16**, read the text below and think of the word which best fits each gap. Use only **one** word in each gap. There is an example at the beginning (**0**).

Write your answers **IN CAPITAL LETTERS on the separate answer sheet**.

Example: | 0 | I | S |

Dolphins on the phone

Did you know it **(0)** .... not just humans who talk? Dolphins do too. And in Hawaii, a female dolphin and her baby have even **(9)** .... a conversation over the telephone! The call was made in an aquarium where the two dolphins swam in separate tanks connected by a special underwater audio link. **(10)** .... they were in different tanks, the two dolphins began whistling and chirping to each **(11)** .... immediately – typical dolphin chatter.

'Information seemed to be passed back **(12)** .... forth very quickly,' explains Don White, a researcher at the aquarium where the experiment took place.

But **(13)** .... exactly were the dolphins saying? **(14)** .... is the question scientists are trying to answer by studying both wild and captive dolphins in the hope that they might **(15)** .... day understand their secret language. They haven't completely cracked the code yet, but they are listening and learning! So who knows? Your next phone call could **(16)** .... from a dolphin!

Part 3

For questions **17–24**, read the text below. Use the word given in capitals at the end of some of the lines to form a word that fits in the gap **in the same line**. There is an example at the beginning (**0**).

Write your answers **IN CAPITAL LETTERS on the separate answer sheet**.

Example: | 0 | S | U | G | G | E | S | T | I | O | N | S | | | | |

Can plants talk?

Have you ever done any gardening? If so, do you have any **(0)** .... **SUGGEST**
on how to speed up and encourage the **(17)** .... of plants? **GROW**
Surprisingly, some gardeners recommend talking or playing music
to them, and now a group of British **(18)** .... have found that this **SCIENCE**
(19) .... may not be quite as crazy as it seems. They discovered **BEHAVE**
that some young plants make a clicking sound in their roots which is so
quiet that humans are unable to hear it. The researchers used special
(20) .... to capture these noises; then when they played the **EQUIP**
(21) .... back to other young plants, they made an amazing **RECORD**
(22) .... – the plants actually grew towards the noise. This seems **DISCOVER**
to suggest that plants can communicate with each other in a way that
experts were previously **(23)** .... of. **AWARE**

It could be that sounds and vibrations are used by plants to share
(24) .... information about growing conditions or about possible **VALUE**
dangers from pests. Perhaps more people should try talking to
their plants!

Part 4

For questions **25–30**, complete the second sentence so that it has a similar meaning to the first sentence, using the word given. **Do not change the word given.** You must use between **two** and **five** words, including the word given. Here is an example (**0**).

Example:

0   Prizes are given out when the school year finishes.

   PLACE

   Prize-giving .... end of each school year.

The gap can be filled by the words 'takes place at the', so you write:

Example: | **0** | TAKES PLACE AT THE |

Write **only** the missing words **IN CAPITAL LETTERS on the separate answer sheet**.

---

25   The bike is quite old so you should ask someone to check the brakes before you ride it.

   GET

   This bike is quite old so you should ………………………………………….. before you ride it.

26   I borrowed my sister's car because I hadn't yet saved enough money to buy my own.

   UNTIL

   My sister ………………………………………….. I had saved enough money to buy my own.

27   I was late for school because I couldn't find my bag.

   TIME

   I ………………………………………….. for school if I'd been able to find my bag.

28   Nicky is the only person who has signed up for the trip.

   NOBODY

   Apart ………………………………………….. their name down for the trip.

29 I regret not listening to my teacher today.

WISH

I ……………………………………….. attention to my teacher today.

30 'I'm very sorry but we haven't got any more chocolate ice cream,' said the waiter.

RUN

'I'm very sorry but we ……………………………………….. chocolate ice cream,' said the waiter.

Part 5

You are going to read an extract from a novel about an American teenager called Bonnie. For questions **31–36**, choose the answer (**A**, **B**, **C** or **D**) which you think fits best according to the text.

Mark your answers **on the separate answer sheet**.

Queen Rider

Bonnie Wyndham got out of her mother's car and looked at Almonside School. 'I'll make you sorry I've come here,' she told her, pleasantly. Her mother was getting out of the other door at the time so she didn't hear, but Bonnie wouldn't have cared if she had. Her mother knew her feelings. Mrs. Wyndham looked about her. Almonside was a funny school, all bits and pieces, buildings hidden away amongst the trees on a wooded hillside; very confusing at first sight. Then she saw the signs on a post: science block, gymnasium, riding centre …

'Riding centre,' said Bonnie, showing a sudden interest.

'Headmaster's study,' said her mother. 'This way.'

Bonnie followed her mother along a broad drive that curved between trees.

'I wish you'd walk beside me instead of following me like a dog,' said Mrs. Wyndham wearily, but she didn't seem to expect Bonnie to do so.

A few minutes later, her mother was talking to Bonnie's new headmaster in his study, while Bonnie herself sat and waited outside the door. Suddenly, Bonnie jumped up. 'Why should I just sit here?' she said to herself. 'I'll be thrown out before very long, anyway,' she said mentally to the door, 'so why not get it over and done with?' She left the building and headed for the riding centre in the direction indicated by the sign.

There was a nice old building where the horses were kept, and a large structure for indoor riding. Bonnie looked about her, but there was no one in sight. There was a certain reverence about her manner as she approached the animals. Bonnie treated horses with respect. The horses were very well looked after, she could tell that at once.

Almost every stall was occupied, and she wandered along looking carefully at each horse and judging it. 'They know what they're doing here,' she told a small pony as she ran a finger along its nose. It was the next horse that pulled her up short. 'But aren't you the best of the lot!' she said. He was brown with a touch of white. Lively, probably, but Bonnie liked that. 'You know, I have the feeling we've met before,' said Bonnie, stroking his neck. 'It was in my dreams and I was riding you to victory in some big competition.' Over the stall was his name: Maverick. *line*

Suddenly, she couldn't resist the temptation to ride the horse. 'I wonder where I can find a bridle for your head, and a saddle for your back. Can't be far away.' The room containing all the riding equipment was – Bonnie was delighted to discover – unlocked. Absorbed in the pleasurable task of putting a saddle on Maverick's back, she forgot all about her mother and the headmaster. When she sat up high on the big horse outside the building, she felt like a queen, mistress of all she could see. Her nickname at her previous school had been Queen Bee, and she laughed delightedly as she remembered it. 'You're the best horse I've ever sat on, Maverick,' she said admiringly, 'and when I say that I'm not kidding, I can assure you, because I know about horses, even if I don't know about anything else.'

She nudged him into a walk, then into a trot. 'If I stay here, I think you and I could be great friends,' she confided. She went round and round the paddock. The rhythm was exhilarating, a little breeze whipping smartly past her cheek and making it glow. She could tell Maverick trusted her, and she felt certain that he'd jump well.

31 What do we learn about Bonnie's mother in the first paragraph?

   A She was used to being obeyed by Bonnie.
   B She had a favourable first impression of the school.
   C She had difficulty finding her way around new places.
   D She was aware of Bonnie's attitude to her new school.

32 Why did Bonnie leave her seat outside the headmaster's office?

   A She was eager to go riding as soon as possible.
   B She was unwilling to spend any time on her own.
   C She didn't think it would make any difference if she behaved badly.
   D She didn't think her mother would take her to see the horses.

33 How did Bonnie feel when she was looking at the horses?

   A excited to recognise a horse she already knew
   B impressed by the high standards at the riding centre
   C anxious to make sure that the horses would like her
   D nervous about being seen with the horses

34 What does 'pulled her up short' mean in line 41?

   A made her stop in surprise
   B made her a bit frightened
   C made her feel sorry
   D made her change her mind

35 When Bonnie was sitting on Maverick's back she felt

   A confident of her riding abilities.
   B determined to prove what she could do.
   C amused that she had tricked her mother.
   D relieved that she had left the past behind.

36 What do we learn about Bonnie by the end of the text?

   A She is looking forward to taking up an exciting hobby.
   B She is concerned about making new friends.
   C She is beginning to feel more positive about the school.
   D She is disappointed about having so little time with the horses.

Part 6

You are going to read an article about two teenagers who send a small model man into space. Six sentences have been removed from the article. Choose from the sentences **A–G** the one which fits each gap (**37–42**). There is one extra sentence which you do not need to use.

Mark your answers **on the separate answer sheet**.

Model man in space

At the young age of 17, Mathew Ho and Asad Muhammad have already sent a man into space – a very small model of a man, that is.

Mathew and Asad attached a four-centimetre-tall model man and four cameras to a balloon and launched the whole thing into space. **37** The boys could hardly believe their success, especially as the entire project had cost them just $400. They had worked on it every weekend for four months. It wasn't a school project; they just thought it would be a cool thing to do. 'We didn't really think it would work until that point,' says Mathew.

Mathew and Asad had the idea for the project two years ago when they saw an online video of a balloon being sent into space by some university students. **38** They both had a passion for all things flight-related so they were the perfect partners for the project.

The pair were soon spending every Saturday at Mathew's house, drawing up plans and building the balloon. 'People would walk in, see us building this weird thing with a parachute, and wonder what we were doing. We'd just say, 'We're sending cameras into space!' Mathew had already made a lightweight box to carry the cameras. **39** They needed ones which could be programmed to take photos every 20 seconds without stopping.

Next they sewed the parachute, which took them three weeks on Asad's mum's sewing machine. 'We soon realised that we're no experts at sewing,' laughs Mathew. 'We broke … what, four needles? Ridiculous!' The end result didn't look too great but worked perfectly. **40** 'People were yelling at us,' remembers Asad.

They ordered a professional weather balloon online, and bought helium gas from a party supply store. Mathew purchased a special wide-angle video camera. Finally, they put the whole thing together, carefully cutting a space inside the lightweight container for three cameras and a mobile phone with a GPS system which helped them to follow it. **41** They also checked with the relevant authorities to make sure its flight wouldn't interfere with air traffic or be illegal.

The boys chose a local football field as their take-off point. Then they blew up the balloon, let it go, and watched their model man float upwards. **42** Less than two hours later, a signal on Mathew's computer told them that the model man had re-entered the earth's atmosphere. He had just landed in a field, 122 kilometres from the launch point. Based on their calculations, the balloon had climbed to about 24,000 metres in just over an hour. Then it exploded, triggering the model man's 32-minute fall to earth. Mathew and Asad have since received a note of congratulations from the manufacturers of the little model man.

A It was just the sort of thing they thought they might be able to do themselves.

B Therefore they needed to calculate where the model would land, based on the take-off point, the weather and the size of the balloon.

C At seven kilometres, they lost both the mobile phone and GPS signals so they went home and made dinner.

D They watched as it landed 97 minutes later, having recorded an astonishing video clip from 24 kilometres above sea level.

E So, with a budget of $500 in mind, they started looking for some which were reasonably priced.

F As a finishing touch, they stuck their model astronaut onto the outside of the box, and found him a tiny national flag to hold.

G They tested it by dropping it off the roof of the building where Mathew lives, which annoyed some of the residents.

Test 1

Part 7

You are going to read an article in which four teenagers talk about part-time work. For questions **43–52**, choose from the teenagers (**A–D**). The teenagers may be chosen more than once.

Mark your answers **on the separate answer sheet**.

Which teenager

argues that having a job encourages people to be more efficient?	43
says there is only a limited range of jobs to choose from?	44
has to put up with people teasing them?	45
hopes to find regular part-time work eventually?	46
puts up with a general disadvantage of having a job?	47
can choose to work less when short of time?	48
got a job to please someone else?	49
doesn't agree with the reason behind someone's decision?	50
was not told off for a mistake they made?	51
did what they could to improve their situation?	52

Saturday jobs

A Keith

I work in a department store on Saturdays, selling men's clothes. My friends mostly work as waiters at the weekend, or deliver newspapers in the mornings before school. They make fun of me because I spend all my time folding shirts. (I'm not particularly fond of doing it.) But I earn a good hourly wage and work in a pleasant environment so I don't care what they say. When I'm older it'll pay for my driving lessons – then I won't need any more lifts to work from Mum. And it's quite flexible – basically, I can give it a miss when I have too much homework. I even have a staff discount card which makes me very popular with my parents! And at the end of each shift, I'm able to buy reduced-price food in the food hall – a big advantage as I'm always hungry!

B James

I wasn't too bothered about getting a Saturday job, but my father talked me into it – he'd done that sort of thing when he was a kid, and he felt he'd learned a great deal that way. So I started looking. I soon found myself spending Saturdays in a local chemist's. The hours were long, and the pay was rubbish, but then I persuaded my friend Tom to join me so it wasn't too bad. It also helped me to get my next job – I now work in a little supermarket round the corner. I think my dad was right – I've become far more independent, and I've learned a lot about people. Some of the customers come in and chat for hours! Like the other people I work with, I have less time to party because I have to get my schoolwork done as well. But when I do go out, I have a bit of money to spend – so it's worth it.

C Caroline

I've never had a part-time job before, but I recently started babysitting for family friends from time to time. It seems to be the most common job among my classmates as it's not badly paid and the kids are nice. One of my friends helps at children's parties, but there doesn't seem to be that much around for teenagers, apart from babysitting. The only other job I've had was as a waitress at a friend's mother's birthday party. I'm pleased to say I only had one incident involving a bowl of soup which I tipped down the side of a sofa, but the people were very reasonable about it. At some point I'd like a better-paid Saturday job, partly to subsidise my ever-increasing collection of clothes, but also for the experience, as I think I could learn a lot from it.

D Freya

I was going to start a Saturday job at a hairdresser's, but Mum changed her mind about it at the last minute, saying I was wrong to risk letting my schoolwork suffer. Working part-time might leave me with less time for schoolwork I suppose, but she overestimates how much time I actually spend on it. Most people I know do something, even if it isn't every week, mainly babysitting for their parents' friends. I think if you work a few hours every week you learn to organise your time better. Now I tend to spend ages on the Internet and chatting to friends. I'm sure I wouldn't do that if I was working – I'd be too busy! But my mum has made her mind up so there's nothing I can do about it.

Test 1

WRITING (1 hour 20 minutes)

Part 1

You **must** answer this question. Write your answer in **140–190** words in an appropriate style.

1   In your English class you have been talking about the best way to spend your free time. Now your English teacher has asked you to write an essay for homework.

Write your essay using **all** the notes and giving reasons for your point of view.

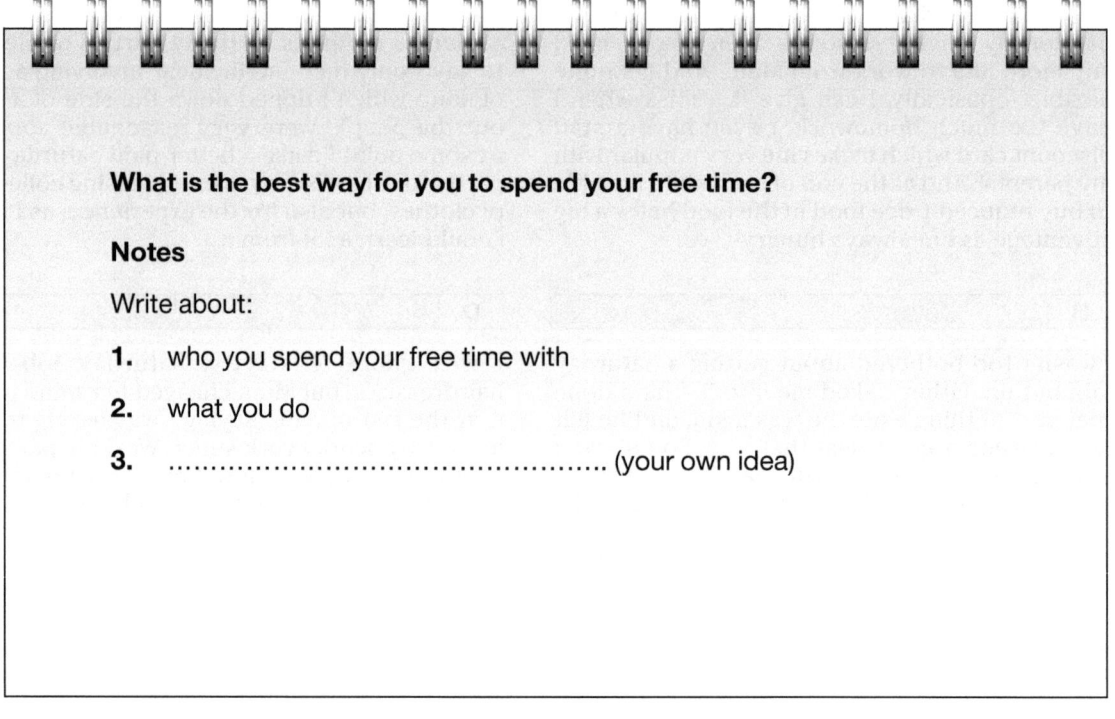

What is the best way for you to spend your free time?

Notes

Write about:

1. who you spend your free time with
2. what you do
3. ………………………………………….. (your own idea)

Part 2

Write an answer to **one** of the questions **2–5** in this part. Write your answer in **140–190** words in an appropriate style **on the separate answer sheet**. Put the question number in the box at the top of the answer sheet.

2   You see this announcement in an international magazine for teenagers.

> **Articles wanted**
>
> **An Interesting Festival**
>
> We are looking for articles about interesting festivals in different countries. Describe one festival in your country and explain what people do. Say why you think it is an interesting festival.
>
> The best articles will appear online next week.

Write your **article**.

3   This is part of a letter you have received from your English friend, Tom.

> As you know, I've been studying science and languages at school for several years now. Next year I have to choose one or the other for my main course of study. Which do you think I should choose and why?
> Write soon,
> Tom

Write your **letter**.

4   You have seen this announcement in a new English-language magazine for schools.

> **Stories wanted**
>
> We are looking for stories for our new English-language magazine for teenagers. Your story must begin with this sentence:
>
> *Lara saw something unusual on the grass and she went to take a closer look.*
>
> Your story must include:
> - a discovery
> - a journey

Write your **story**.

5   Answer the following question based on the title below.

Macbeth by William Shakespeare

Your English class has had a discussion about the characters in the story of *Macbeth*. Now your teacher has asked you to write an essay for homework answering these questions:
- How does the behaviour of Macbeth change during the story?
- Why does this happen?

Write your **essay**.

Test 1

LISTENING (approximately 40 minutes)

Part 1

You will hear people talking in eight different situations. For questions **1–8**, choose the best answer (**A**, **B** or **C**).

1   You hear part of a news item about a school project.
    What have the students at the school invented?

    A   an unusual means of transport

    B   a method of making ice cream

    C   a way of producing energy

2   You hear a teacher talking to her students about a writing competition.
    What is she doing?

    A   encouraging them to go in for it

    B   suggesting how they could do well in it

    C   correcting information they've received about it

3   You hear part of a radio item about a bird.
    The presenter is explaining why

    A   the bird has the appearance it has.

    B   the bird has arrived at a wildlife centre.

    C   the bird was given the name Manukura.

4   You hear two friends talking about a TV talent show.
    What do they agree about?

    A   The girl band made a surprising choice of song.

    B   The singer who ended the show had a very strong voice.

    C   The performers were generally better than in previous weeks.

Listening

5 You hear a girl talking about a sports event she took part in.
What is the girl doing?

    A giving her opinion about people at the event

    B explaining why she did so well in the event

    C describing what happened at the event

6 You hear a teacher telling her class about something called World Oceans Day.
What is the teacher going to do next?

    A give more information about the importance of oceans

    B listen to suggestions about how to celebrate the day

    C say how the class could help the environment

7 You hear an announcement about a festival.
What is the speaker's main purpose?

    A to describe the event

    B to publicise a competition

    C to explain how to get tickets

8 You hear a boy leaving a voicemail message for his friend.
Why is he calling his friend?

    A to offer to do something

    B to complain about something

    C to give advice about something

Test 1

Part 2

You will hear a boy called Joe giving a class presentation about a project he's done on the subject of gorillas. For questions **9–18**, complete the sentences with a word or short phrase.

Gorillas

The thing that first got Joe interested in gorillas was a [_____ **9**_____] he saw as a child.

Joe's uncle saw gorillas in the south of Uganda whilst working as a [_____ **10**_____] there.

The species Joe's uncle saw in Uganda were [_____ **11**_____] gorillas.

Joe used a website called [_____ **12**_____].com as the main source of information for his project.

Joe uses the word [_____ **13**_____] to describe the way that gorillas usually behave.

Joe discovered that, as well as vegetation, [_____ **14**_____] sometimes form part of the gorilla's diet.

The name [_____ **15**_____] is used to refer to the young males in a group.

Joe says that gorillas choose the [_____ **16**_____] as the place to build their nests.

Joe explains that [_____ **17**_____] are the main threat to gorillas.

Joe recommends a book entitled *Gorillas in the* [_____ **18**_____] for finding out more about them.

Part 3

You will hear five short extracts in which teenagers are talking about a recent holiday. For questions **19–23**, choose from the list (**A–H**) the opinion each speaker expresses. Use the letters only once. There are three extra letters which you do not need to use.

A   The best bit was meeting someone who's become a close friend.

B   I was good at an activity I hadn't tried before.

Speaker 1	19

C   I had a great time performing in a musical event.

Speaker 2	20

D   A new experience was more enjoyable than I'd expected.

Speaker 3	21

E   The journey to our destination was my favourite part.

Speaker 4	22

F   I was proud that I could speak the local language.

Speaker 5	23

G   It was more exciting than previous visits to the same place.

H   It was good to go away with people for the first time.

Test 1

Part 4

You will hear an interview with a writer called Clare Watson, who writes novels for teenagers. For questions **24–30**, choose the best answer (**A**, **B** or **C**).

24 What first made Clare want to become a novelist?

  A the encouragement of a teacher

  B her own passion for reading

  C positive feedback from her brother

25 Clare says that her favourite novel

  A turned out as she hoped it would.

  B is more amusing than her others.

  C is the first in a series.

26 Where does Clare get the ideas for her stories?

  A They often have their origins in her dreams.

  B They come to her when she's exercising.

  C They appear when she least expects them.

27 How does Clare feel about the TV series that features one of her characters?

  A She wishes it had been made years ago.

  B She's glad that other people write the scripts.

  C She thinks the actors have been well chosen.

28 What inspired Clare to set up writing groups?

    A a conversation with other authors

    B letters she received from readers

    C a similar project she heard about

29 How did Clare feel when she won an award?

    A honoured because her favourite writer had won it before

    B apprehensive about how it might change her life

    C surprised because she didn't feel she was the best

30 Clare says she can write well about how teenagers feel because

    A she's got very clear memories of herself at that age.

    B she's in regular contact with teenage relatives.

    C she spent several years of her life as a teacher.

Test 1

SPEAKING (14 minutes)

You take the Speaking test with another candidate (possibly two candidates), referred to here as your partner. There are two examiners. One will speak to you and your partner and the other will be listening. Both examiners will award marks.

Part 1 (2 minutes)

The examiner asks you and your partner questions about yourselves. You may be asked about things like 'your home town', 'your interests', 'your career plans', etc.

Part 2 (a one-minute 'long turn' for each candidate, plus a 20-second response from the second candidate)

The examiner gives you two photographs and asks you to talk about them for one minute. The examiner then asks your partner a question about your photographs and your partner responds briefly.

Then the examiner gives your partner two different photographs. Your partner talks about these photographs for one minute. This time the examiner asks you a question about your partner's photographs and you respond briefly.

Part 3 (4 minutes)

The examiner asks you and your partner to talk together. You may be asked to solve a problem or try to come to a decision about something. For example, you might be asked to decide the best way to use some rooms in a language school. The examiner gives you some text to help you but does not join in the conversation.

Part 4 (4 minutes)

The examiner asks some further questions, which leads to a more general discussion of what you have talked about in Part 3. You may comment on your partner's answers if you wish.

Test 2

Test 2

READING AND USE OF ENGLISH (1 hour 15 minutes)

Part 1

For questions **1–8**, read the text below and decide which answer (**A, B, C** or **D**) best fits each gap. There is an example at the beginning (**0**).

Mark your answers **on the separate answer sheet**.

Example:

0 **A** managed   **B** arrived   **C** succeeded   **D** reached

| 0 | A ■ | B ▢ | C ▢ | D ▢ |

Captain of a team

What are the secrets of success in sport? After winning a big match, players are often asked how they **(0)** …….. to do it. Most say it is the result of hard work and practice. But another important **(1)** …….. in their success is their team captain. The players **(2)** …….. on the captain to motivate them and **(3)** …….. they all play well together as a team. The role of captain only **(4)** …….. a person who works well under pressure. Could you be a captain? Can you take **(5)** …….. of a group of people, even when they are tired or frustrated? Can you ensure that the team achieves its full **(6)** …….. during a match? It's not easy, but those who do this well are rewarded with a team of players who respect them and **(7)** …….. them. **(8)** …….. they may not win every match, they will do everything they can to make the captain proud of them. That's the secret of success.

30

1	**A** feature	**B** factor	**C** mark	**D** characteristic
2	**A** rely	**B** trust	**C** believe	**D** hope
3	**A** prepare	**B** provide	**C** enable	**D** ensure
4	**A** fits	**B** suits	**C** matches	**D** applies
5	**A** direction	**B** order	**C** responsibility	**D** charge
6	**A** talent	**B** ability	**C** potential	**D** promise
7	**A** catch up with	**B** look up to	**C** come up with	**D** get up to
8	**A** However	**B** Despite	**C** Although	**D** Even

Part 2

For questions **9–16**, read the text below and think of the word which best fits each gap. Use only **one** word in each gap. There is an example at the beginning (**0**).

Write your answers **IN CAPITAL LETTERS on the separate answer sheet**.

Example: | 0 | M | O | R | E | | | | | | | | | | | |

Horses

Surprisingly, there are **(0)** .... than 350 different breeds of horse around the world. Many of them can live for up **(9)** .... 30 years. A male horse is called a gelding or a stallion, and a female horse is **(10)** .... as a mare. The height of a horse is measured in 'hands', a hand being the distance **(11)** .... a man's wrist to the tip of his middle finger. The tallest horse ever recorded was Sampson, who lived in the 1850s and stood at over 21 hands.

Horses use facial expressions to communicate emotions. If you know **(12)** .... to look for, their nostrils, eyes and ears will help you to interpret their feelings. Their eyes are positioned on the sides of their head, enabling them to see behind them and making **(13)** .... easier for them to detect predators. They also have the ability to turn **(14)** .... ears from side to side, **(15)** .... is particularly important for wild horses because they need to know where danger is **(16)** .... from.

Reading and Use of English

Part 3

For questions **17–24**, read the text below. Use the word given in capitals at the end of some of the lines to form a word that fits in the gap **in the same line**. There is an example at the beginning (**0**).

Write your answers I**N CAPITAL LETTERS** on the separate answer sheet.

Example: | 0 | O | B | V | I | O | U | S | L | Y | | | | | | |

Fun with science

So you think science is boring? Well, you have **(0)** .... never been on one of our Mad Science courses! We run classes which are designed to wake up your imagination and also develop your **(17)** .... of how the world around you works. Working in teams, or **(18)** .... if you prefer, you get the chance to try a whole range of experiments and then build your own robot to take home at the end of the day. Each group of young scientists has a set of **(19)** .... to work from, and tutors are there to help if anything is at all **(20)** ....

OBVIOUS

UNDERSTAND
INDIVIDUAL

INSTRUCT
CLEAR

The activities are so **(21)** .... that you will forget that they are also **(22)** .... ! Our courses run all day, from 10 am to 5 pm and are held at several different **(23)** .... around the country. The courses are very popular and **(24)** .... is limited so make sure you book early!

ENJOY
EDUCATION
LOCATE
AVAILABLE

33

Test 2

Part 4

For questions **25–30**, complete the second sentence so that it has a similar meaning to the first sentence, using the word given. **Do not change the word given**. You must use between **two** and **five** words, including the word given. Here is an example (0).

Example:

0   Prizes are given out when the school year finishes.

   PLACE

   Prize-giving .... end of each school year.

The gap can be filled by the words 'takes place at the', so you write:

| **Example:** | **0** | *TAKES PLACE AT THE* |

Write **only** the missing words **IN CAPITAL LETTERS** on the separate answer sheet.

---

25   I'd like to be an actor one day but fame doesn't interest me.

   INTERESTED

   I'd like to be an actor one day but I'm .... famous.

26   I didn't go skating because I was too tired.

   WOULD

   I .... I hadn't been so tired.

27   It's been absolutely ages since I last saw David.

   SEEN

   I .... absolutely ages.

28   Can you tell me the difference between these two computers?

   DIFFERENT

   Can you tell me how .... from that one?

29 It was windy and raining but we still went to the beach.

SPITE

We went to the beach ………………………………………….. and rain.

30 Dad had bought everything we needed before I arrived at the supermarket.

GOT

By the ……………………………………….. supermarket, Dad had bought everything we needed.

Part 5

You are going to read an extract from a novel about a Canadian teenager called Rex. For questions **31–36**, choose the answer (**A**, **B**, **C** or **D**) which you think fits best according to the text.

Mark your answers **on the separate answer sheet**.

Kayak Rex

I leapt from my bed, lifted a corner of the bedroom curtain, and looked down on the river bend. A fresh crack in the ice glistened in the morning sunlight. I shaded my eyes and looked upstream towards the wall of sandbags, there to protect the buildings from flooding as the river ice melted. My back still ached from lifting them into place. All last week, I'd worked alongside most of the town's adult population for long hours, proving I was up to the task. Not that my grandfather took much notice.

With one hand still on the curtain, I swept my eyes along the half-mile ribbon of steaming black water formed by the release pipe from the wood processing factory in Milltown. With fragile ice shelves on either side, the dark open patch was followed by solid ice downstream. As I took off my pyjamas and reached for my kayaking wetsuit, I spotted a boy on the far side of the river's edge – a boy I didn't recognise. I frowned. Unbelievably, he was attempting to balance on an ice shelf along the water warmed by the factory. I zipped up my wetsuit and reached for my kayaking jacket. I checked the pocket for the lucky chain I keep there – a silver chain my famous grandfather once brought back from an expedition in South America. Far better than having a famous grandfather is having this chain, which no one but him, my mom and me know about. Plus, I have the actual diary that he kept on that journey. I keep it under my pillow and read bits of it before I fall asleep. I patted the chain again and made my way towards the kitchen.

line 19

'Morning, Rex.' Mom smiled at me as I grabbed a banana off the kitchen counter. 'You're up early for a Saturday. I'll cook up brunch after your training session. Be careful now.' 'Thanks, Mom.' I headed down the hallway, nearly slamming into Grandpa's tall thin frame as he stepped out of his bedroom. 'Can't you ever watch where you're going?' he shouted. 'Where are you going, anyway?' 'Sorry, Grandpa. I'm going kayaking.' As if my wetsuit didn't make that obvious. As if he didn't see me in my kayak every morning. Grandpa is Grandpa, and I try to ignore it when he loses his temper, but he's been making it that much harder for me to do lately.

'What's the point of training? You didn't win the competition,' he said. For a split second, the steel-edged remark hit exactly like he meant it to. But I took a deep breath and silently counted to three. He crossed the hall and slammed the bathroom door shut behind him. Mom appeared with a sympathetic smile. 'Don't mind him. He's …' '… not himself at the moment,' I finished for her. I refrained from saying that he'd always been that way. But, like Mom, I try to go easy on him.

When I was a child, he was my hero – from the time he first showed me photos of him in the *National Geographic* magazine. Those faded photos still hang framed on his bedroom wall, above his dust-covered expedition medals and trophies. But I don't go into his room anymore. I've got my own growing collection of trophies to look at and, someday soon, maybe, my own face in *National Geographic*. And yet, well, a part of me still wants to remain devoted to him, this ill-tempered old man.

Mom smiled. 'At least, he's coming out of his bedroom more. Have a good session, Rex. I admire your determination to keep it up, even on these cold days!' I smiled back at her as I peeled my banana. 'It'll be warmer in South America,' I said. 'If I come up with sponsors for my expedition.' She laughed and returned to the kitchen. I ate my banana and went downstairs. Stepping into the backyard, I hurried towards the boathouse.

31 How did Rex feel as he looked at the sandbags?

    A satisfied with the work he had done
    B eager to get down to the river
    C relieved that the flooding was over
    D concerned he might have to move them again

32 When Rex 'frowned' in line 19, it showed that

    A he wished he were outside with the boy.
    B he was trying to remember the boy's name.
    C he disapproved of the boy's actions.
    D he was unable to make out what the boy was doing.

33 What do we learn about Rex's grandfather in the third paragraph?

    A He has little idea of what is going on.
    B He is behaving increasingly badly.
    C He needs more and more attention.
    D He is often in the way.

34 How did Rex react to his grandfather's comment about the competition?

    A He decided that his grandfather hadn't intended to hurt him.
    B He wanted to reply to his grandfather but wasn't sure what to say.
    C He hoped to annoy his grandfather by pretending he hadn't heard.
    D He ignored his grandfather despite feeling upset about the criticism.

35 In the fifth paragraph, what is suggested about Rex's attitude to his grandfather?

    A Rex has always felt the need to compete with his grandfather.
    B Rex believes his grandfather exaggerates his past achievements.
    C Rex is sad about the way his relationship with his grandfather has changed.
    D Rex feels guilty because he is already more successful than his grandfather was.

36 At the end of the passage, what are we told about Rex?

    A He is receiving support to go on an exciting trip.
    B He trains regularly whatever the weather is like.
    C He gets little encouragement from his mother.
    D He is planning to move somewhere less cold.

Part 6

You are going to read an article about a ball that can generate electricity. Six sentences have been removed from the article. Choose from the sentences **A–G** the one which fits each gap (**37–42**). There is one extra sentence which you do not need to use.

Mark your answers **on the separate answer sheet**.

Need electricity? Play a game of soccer!

Two inventors have produced a new soccer ball called 'Soccket' that can generate electricity.

Though 25% of the world's population may not have easy access to electricity, we all have access to a source of energy that is currently being wasted – energy released by our bodies when we move around. Two inventors have figured out how to capture this energy and convert it into electricity. The only equipment needed? A Soccket football and the desire to have some fun.

The story behind this amazing invention began at an unusual engineering class where non-engineers were challenged to combine art and science, and come up with a practical solution to help the world. Two students – Julia Silverman and Jessica Mathews – decided to give it a try. The pair discussed issues facing many people around the world to see which of them they could help tackle. **37**

That's when Julia, who used to play a lot of sports in high school, had a brilliant idea: what if they were able to capture some of the energy that is generated when people play sports? **38** Given its popularity among both young and old all over the world, soccer seemed to be the natural sport of choice, and the ball the perfect thing to do it with!

The innovative idea won their professor's approval. It then became the passion and life goal of these two young women. After graduating, they founded Uncharted Play, Inc., a non-profit-making company. **39**

They tried their idea out at home first by sticking a shake-to-charge flashlight they had bought inside a small, hollow ball. Then they kicked it around to see if the flashlight would pick up the charge. **40** A mechanism inside the ball captured the energy created as the ball moved, which could then be converted into electricity. They made a number of these balls which were tested by delighted kids at the World Cup Soccer Championships. Just under 150g heavier than a regulation soccer ball, the Soccket had the capacity to store enough energy to power up a small lamp for three hours following just 30 minutes of play.

The company then worked on the first Soccket football to be produced in large numbers. The latest model is six to seven times more energy efficient than the original, and has the capacity to store enough energy to power a reading lamp, a cell phone charger and even a water purifier. **41** The company encourages people not only to buy one for themselves but also to donate one to a country where it might be needed.

And the Soccket is not the young entrepreneurs' only idea – having succeeded with the Soccket, they have many similar ideas combining fun and function. **42** As Silverman says: 'Just because we get older doesn't mean we have to stop playing, and just because we need important things in our life, like electricity, doesn't mean we can't have fun producing them.'

A The version they produced after that was a little more sophisticated.

B Of course, they plan to develop these.

C In this way, the ball could produce even more electricity.

D Maybe they could convert it into electricity.

E Access to cheap electricity was one that came to mind right away.

F This was the first version to become available worldwide.

G They hoped it would help to improve many people's lives.

Test 2

Part 7

You are going to read four reviews of school concerts. For questions **43–52**, choose from the reviews (**A–D**). The reviews may be chosen more than once.

Mark your answers **on the separate answer sheet**.

Which review writer

is looking forward to hearing the players on another occasion?	43
heard some popular pieces performed in a modern way?	44
says a performance involved a risk that paid off?	45
says a performance was as good as people thought it would be?	46
predicts successful careers for some performers?	47
says the students played more difficult pieces than they normally do?	48
mentions how hard everybody worked before the concert?	49
was impressed by the performers' ability to concentrate?	50
admits that some of the music didn't appeal to them?	51
wishes one performance had been longer?	52

School concert reviews

A Garston High School

Garston High School's annual concert took place in the sports hall last Wednesday. The enthusiasm of the players and their teachers, combined with many hours of rehearsals, produced a varied and enjoyable show, as it does every year. The concert opened with the Garston High School Orchestra, whose expert playing lived up to all expectations. They were followed by the school choir with a dynamic performance of the song, 'Going Places', complete with hand claps, that was much appreciated. Janie Evans' flute solo provided a quiet, peaceful moment, rapidly followed by the choir again with contemporary versions of several well-known favourites. Garston's jazz band then took to the stage, and the audience were soon tapping their feet happily to the lively rhythms. The concert ended with the orchestra in a final inspiring performance. All in all, it was a thoroughly enjoyable evening.

B Hartisford School

Hartisford School's music department has never been regarded as anything special, but after last night's concert that may all be about to change. The college orchestra, unlike in previous years, performed music that challenged musicians, moving away from the more traditional pieces parents and families have become used to. Although at times this proved slightly too ambitious, they deserve credit for trying to aim high. Some of the solo pieces went on for a little too long, but others were entertaining. The students have some hard work to do, but they will no doubt be helped by the new staff at Hartisford. I'm making sure I don't miss their end-of-year concert which I know will be well worth going to.

C Ruttler's School

Some of the students currently attending Ruttler's School are remarkably talented musicians, and it was a pleasure to be in the audience at their concert on Friday. The first solo performance was by Dan Smith, a talented pianist who also played the violin in the orchestra. Next came Emma Jordan on drums, who was brave enough to perform a fast-moving modern piece which even very accomplished professionals might hesitate to play in public. The audience rewarded her by clapping and cheering for several minutes, which she thoroughly deserved. The musicians in the school rock band were on excellent form, though they did play a few numbers that weren't entirely to my taste. The concert finished with all the performers and their teachers on stage at once, playing 'Gotta Go', which was the perfect end to the evening.

D Summerford School

Summerford School's spring concert yesterday was a great success, despite irritating interruptions from mobile phones. The players and singers are to be congratulated for not allowing this to interfere with the performance. The tightly-packed programme gave students an opportunity to show off the range of their talent, and there were so many excellent performances that it would be impossible for me to list them all here. Sarah Liddell on guitar, however, deserves a mention. I was disappointed when her solo ended, as I'd been looking forward to hearing her play. Liam Hunter's piano playing was also outstanding. Another highlight was the string quartet, featuring four very talented young people who will no doubt achieve great things one day. Once again, Summerford School has provided a fantastic evening's entertainment.

Test 2

WRITING (1 hour 20 minutes)

Part 1

You **must** answer this question. Write your answer in **140–190** words in an appropriate style.

1 In your English class you have been comparing large and small schools. Now your English teacher has asked you to write an essay for homework.

Write your essay using **all** the notes and giving reasons for your point of view.

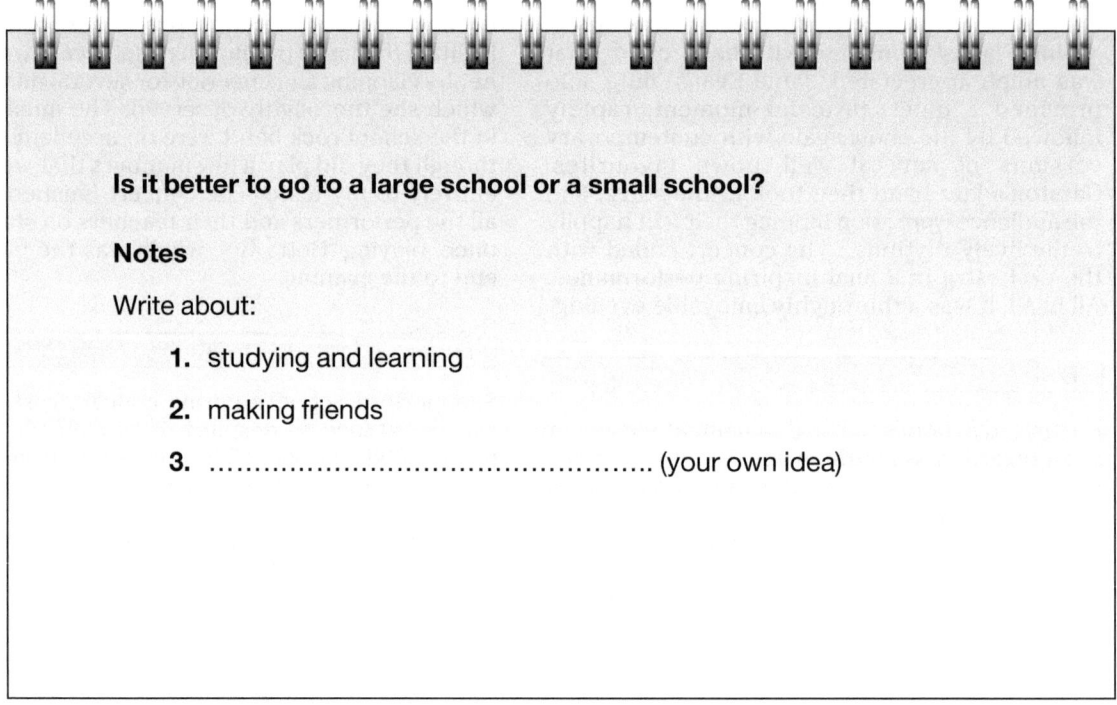

Is it better to go to a large school or a small school?

Notes

Write about:

1. studying and learning
2. making friends
3. ………………………………………….. (your own idea)

Writing

Part 2

Write an answer to **one** of the questions **2–5** in this part. Write your answer in **140–190** words in an appropriate style **on the separate answer sheet**. Put the question number in the box at the top of the answer sheet.

2 You see this announcement in your school magazine.

> **Articles wanted**
>
> ## Finding time to keep fit and healthy
>
> How do you manage to keep fit and healthy as well as study and spend time with your friends?
>
> Write an article telling us what you think. Write about the food you eat, the exercise you take, and anything else you think is important.
>
> The best articles will be published in next month's school magazine.

Write your **article**.

3 You have received this email from your Australian friend, Sarah.

> We're doing a project in our class about where young people in different countries go for their holidays. Where do **you** usually go for your holidays and what do you do there? Do you enjoy this kind of holiday?
> Thanks for your help!
> Sarah

Write your **email**.

4 You recently saw this notice in an English-language magazine for teenagers.

> **Reviews wanted**
>
> ### A Good Café to Meet Friends in!
>
> We're doing a guide about cafés where teenagers can go to meet friends and relax. Tell us about a café you know. Write about where it is, the kind of food it serves and the atmosphere there. Tell us why you think other people your age would like it.
>
> The best reviews will be published next month.

Write your **review**.

5 Answer the following question based on the title below.

Touching the Void by Joe Simpson

Your English book club is looking for reviews of adventure stories. Write a review of *Touching the Void*, saying why you would recommend it.

Write your **review**.

Test 2

LISTENING (approximately 40 minutes)

Part 1

You will hear people talking in eight different situations. For questions **1–8**, choose the best answer (**A**, **B** or **C**).

1   You hear a teacher talking to some students.
    What is he doing?

    A   explaining the benefits of walking holidays

    B   emphasising the natural beauty of some places

    C   describing the difference between two areas

2   You hear two friends talking about a bike race they went on.
    What does the girl say about it?

    A   She was disappointed with her speed.

    B   She found it more difficult than expected.

    C   She almost gave up before the finish.

3   You hear a man and his daughter talking in a library.
    What is the man doing?

    A   recommending a book for his daughter to read

    B   complaining about his daughter's reading habits

    C   promising to help his daughter to choose a book

4   You hear two friends talking about a television programme about polar bears.
    What do they both think was unusual about it?

    A   the information given in it

    B   the location chosen for it

    C   the skill involved in filming it

5 You hear a teacher talking to a class.
What does she want her students to do this week?

    A bring some items to school

    B find out some information

    C make something at home

6 You hear two friends talking about a story-writing competition.
They agree that they will

    A each write a story and go in for it.

    B share the prize if one of them wins it.

    C visit a zoo together to get ideas for it.

7 You hear a radio announcement about an event.
What is the aim of the event?

    A to encourage young people to get involved in science

    B to raise city residents' awareness of unusual wildlife

    C to find out about trends in animal numbers

8 You hear a review of a computer game on the radio.
What does the reviewer think of the game?

    A It is surprisingly different from other adventure games.

    B It is likely to have a very broad appeal to computer gamers.

    C It is only suitable for people experienced in this type of game.

Test 2

Part 2

You will hear a girl called Kate giving a class presentation on the subject of chocolate. For questions **9–18**, complete the sentences with a word or short phrase.

Chocolate

Hundreds of years ago, people known as the Mayans added hot peppers and [9] to cocoa beans to make the first chocolate drink.

Kate explains that ancient Mayan people started growing cocoa trees in [10] as chocolate became popular in their culture.

The Aztecs used cocoa beans rather than [11] to settle their debts.

Kate mentions that Spanish explorers brought the [12] to Europe before the cocoa bean.

In the 17th century, the [13] was introduced to protect people's clothes when they drank chocolate.

In 1795, an English company called J. Fry and Sons invented a machine driven by [14] which was used to grind the cocoa beans.

A special machine for making solid chocolate called a [15] was developed in 1828.

In 1847, chocolate [16] began to be produced by an English company.

In 1875, a man from Switzerland called Daniel Peter added [17] to chocolate.

Recent research shows that chocolate can improve people's [18] .

Part 3

You will hear five short extracts in which teenagers are talking about a family day out at an activity centre. For questions **19–23**, choose from the list (**A–H**) what each speaker says about the place they went to. Use the letters only once. There are three extra letters which you do not need to use.

A I bought something useful at the shop.

B I've been given a good reason to go back regularly.

Speaker 1 [ ] **19**

C I enjoy the idea of being independent of my parents.

Speaker 2 [ ] **20**

D I didn't need to take advantage of the help that was available.

Speaker 3 [ ] **21**

E I was able to practise a skill I've been learning elsewhere.

Speaker 4 [ ] **22**

F I didn't manage to do everything I wanted to do.

Speaker 5 [ ] **23**

G I'd be keen to find out more about the place.

H I'd like to do the same activity somewhere nearer home.

Test 2

Part 4

You will hear an interview with a girl called Poppy Wallace, who sings in a girl band called GirlSong. For questions **24–30**, choose the best answer (**A**, **B** or **C**).

24 What does Poppy say about the band's success this year?

   A The girls didn't expect it to happen so quickly.

   B The girls haven't had enough time to appreciate it.

   C The girls recognise that it was the result of years of hard work.

25 How does Poppy feel about GirlSong's recent tour?

   A glad to have spent time with the fans

   B pleased that it's made them more confident performers

   C happy with the way relationships within the band have developed

26 How did GirlSong come to work with the singer called Leo?

   A Their agent contacted him about it.

   B He suggested it after hearing their music.

   C They met him by chance at a recording studio.

27 What is Poppy's attitude to working with Leo again?

   A She's alarmed about the attention they will get.

   B She's excited about the opportunity to perform with him.

   C She's concerned about the pressure involved.

28 On international tours, Poppy likes to

   A make time for seeing the local sights.

   B try singing local folk songs.

   C learn simple phrases in the local language.

29 What does Poppy enjoy most when she visits Barbados?

    A eating the island's food

    B playing music with friends

    C relaxing on the beach

30 Who did Poppy admire most as a child?

    A a singer whose songs she identified with

    B a teacher whose lessons inspired her

    C a film character whose behaviour appealed to her

SPEAKING (14 minutes)

You take the Speaking test with another candidate (possibly two candidates), referred to here as your partner. There are two examiners. One will speak to you and your partner and the other will be listening. Both examiners will award marks.

Part 1 (2 minutes)

The examiner asks you and your partner questions about yourselves. You may be asked about things like 'your home town', 'your interests', 'your career plans', etc.

Part 2 (a one-minute 'long turn' for each candidate, plus a 20-second response from the second candidate)

The examiner gives you two photographs and asks you to talk about them for one minute. The examiner then asks your partner a question about your photographs and your partner responds briefly.

Then the examiner gives your partner two different photographs. Your partner talks about these photographs for one minute. This time the examiner asks you a question about your partner's photographs and you respond briefly.

Part 3 (4 minutes)

The examiner asks you and your partner to talk together. You may be asked to solve a problem or try to come to a decision about something. For example, you might be asked to decide the best way to use some rooms in a language school. The examiner gives you some text to help you but does not join in the conversation.

Part 4 (4 minutes)

The examiner asks some further questions, which leads to a more general discussion of what you have talked about in Part 3. You may comment on your partner's answers if you wish.

Test 3

Test 3

READING AND USE OF ENGLISH (1 hour 15 minutes)

Part 1

For questions **1–8**, read the text below and decide which answer (**A**, **B**, **C** or **D**) best fits each gap. There is an example at the beginning (**0**).

Mark your answers **on the separate answer sheet**.

Example:

0   **A** trying   **B** doing   **C** finding   **D** carrying

| 0 | A ▬ | B ▭ | C ▭ | D ▭ |

Testing games

How lucky can you be? Twelve-year-old Eloise Noakes has got the best job in the world – **(0)** …….. out new games. A **(1)** …….. company held a competition to find young testers and Eloise was selected to test games which are about to be **(2)** …….. onto the market. Each week she is given a different game to play before **(3)** …….. her thoughts on a form designed by the company. As the company director said, 'What better way to find out about games than to put them in the hands of the customers who will make most **(4)** …….. of them?' Eloise is **(5)** …….. with her new job but she also takes it very **(6)** …….. . She is allowed to keep the games after testing them, but she has decided instead to give them **(7)** …….. to children less fortunate than herself. 'I've got **(8)** …….. of games and some children don't have any,' she explained.

52

1	**A** primary	**B** chief	**C** superior	**D** leading
2	**A** sold	**B** launched	**C** promoted	**D** sent
3	**A** signing	**B** copying	**C** recording	**D** filling
4	**A** use	**B** value	**C** practice	**D** worth
5	**A** amused	**B** delighted	**C** thankful	**D** proud
6	**A** calmly	**B** deeply	**C** thoroughly	**D** seriously
7	**A** back	**B** over	**C** away	**D** in
8	**A** plenty	**B** many	**C** enough	**D** several

Part 2

For questions **9–16**, read the text below and think of the word which best fits each gap. Use only **one** word in each gap. There is an example at the beginning (**0**).

Write your answers **IN CAPITAL LETTERS on the separate answer sheet**.

Example: | 0 | O | N | E | | | | | | | | | | | | |

Reading is good for you

Reading really is **(0)** .... of the best hobbies you can have. **(9)** .... only is it entertaining, but it also improves your mind; when you're reading, you're frequently having **(10)** .... work things out, so you're actively using your brain. And you often come **(11)** .... new words, so it's good for improving your vocabulary too.

Another benefit of reading is that it develops your memory. If you're reading detective fiction, for example, you'll find **(12)** .... hard to follow the story **(13)** .... you can remember all the little details which are essential to the plot. Moreover, people who read a lot tend to **(14)** .... more imaginative because they're exposed to new ideas, and this helps to develop the creative side of the brain. It might also boost your confidence because reading can increase your general knowledge – you'll always have **(15)** .... interesting to talk about! So what are you waiting for? **(16)** .... reading a try!

Part 3

For questions **17–24**, read the text below. Use the word given in capitals at the end of some of the lines to form a word that fits in the gap **in the same line**. There is an example at the beginning (**0**).

Write your answers **IN CAPITAL LETTERS** on the separate answer sheet.

Example: | 0 | S | O | C | I | E | T | Y | | | | | | | |

Outward Bound

Have you ever wanted to hike up a mountain, sleep in a boat or spend a day completely cut off from modern **(0)** .... , but didn't because you were **(17)** .... to give it a try? Well, now you can turn your dreams into reality on an Outward Bound programme. We run courses all over the world which are designed to improve people's **(18)** .... of the great outdoors and to experience things that it would be **(19)** .... to experience in their **(20)** .... lives. But an Outward Bound course is not only about adventure, it is a journey of **(21)** .... , during which you learn about yourself and others. The activities teach you valuable lessons about your own strengths and **(22)** .... and along the way you will form many new **(23)** .... The days you spend on an Outward Bound course will help you to find out who you really are and what you want to be. So why not join us? It could be one of the best **(24)** .... you will ever make!

SOCIAL
FRIGHT

KNOW
POSSIBLE
DAY
DISCOVER

WEAK
FRIEND

DECIDE

Part 4

For questions **25–30**, complete the second sentence so that it has a similar meaning to the first sentence, using the word given. **Do not change the word given.** You must use between **two** and **five** words, including the word given. Here is an example (**0**).

Example:

0   Prizes are given out when the school year finishes.

   PLACE

   Prize-giving .... end of each school year.

The gap can be filled by the words 'takes place at the', so you write:

Example: | **0** | *TAKES PLACE AT THE* |

Write **only** the missing words **IN CAPITAL LETTERS on the separate answer sheet**.

---

25   It's a pity I didn't see Jane before she went on holiday.

   WISH

   I .... Jane before she went on holiday.

26   Richard only arrived just before the concert began.

   TURN

   Richard .... until just before the concert began.

27   Despite not feeling well, Lisa went to the cinema with her friends.

   ALTHOUGH

   Lisa went to the cinema with her friends .... well.

28   When does the bus leave on Sundays?

   WHAT

   Can you tell me .... on Sundays?

29 This computer package includes all the software.

INCLUDED

All the software ………………………………………….. this computer package.

30 My teacher let me leave the lesson early because I wasn't feeling well.

ALLOWED

I ………………………………………….. the lesson early because I wasn't feeling well.

Part 5

You are going to read a magazine article about a young mountain climber. For questions **31–36**, choose the answer (**A**, **B**, **C** or **D**) which you think fits best according to the text.

Mark your answers **on the separate answer sheet**.

Teenage Climber

Kai Bradey is 14 and plans to be one of the youngest people ever to climb Mount Everest. Kai's team for the climb includes his father, Ed, and mother, Melissa. They call themselves 'The Bradey Team', and climbing Everest is only one part of their plan. If Kai succeeds in climbing Everest, and Koscuiszko in Australia, he will become one of the youngest people to have climbed the Seven Summits, the highest points on each continent. Few people achieve this under the age of thirty. Kai has already climbed four of them and might actually do it before his teenage years are over. If he makes it, he could become one of the most famous teens of his generation. Because young people are spending more time on computers and games consoles, Kai hopes to inspire kids to climb their own mountains. Or, at least, to venture outdoors.

line 12

I have spoken to a number of well-known Everest climbers and could not find a single one who thought that taking a 14-year-old up the world's highest mountain was a good idea. They questioned whether many young climbers had the necessary physical strength, and had doubts about whether a teenager would be prepared emotionally for the challenge. In addition, they couldn't see how a young person could have gained enough practical knowledge or awareness of potential hazards to develop the good judgment and reactions a climber must have in order to take part in such a project safely.

The Bradeys have heard such views before. 'I know that people are critical of us – I have to put up with that,' Ed says, 'but I don't waste my time thinking about it – there's still so much to do. I think about possible problems, obviously. Melissa and I weigh up the risks all the time. I'm concerned for Kai's safety as any parent would be, but I believe our own backgound as climbers will help, and watching Kai develop gives me confidence.'

I also wonder about Kai's motivation. Is this just an ambitious father taking his own love of adventure to a dangerous extreme? 'This project isn't about me trying to become famous for my son's achievements,' Ed insists. 'At first, he talked about it as something for later in life, but when we discussed it, we thought: 'Why wait?' We talk to him from time to time to make sure he hasn't lost the motivation to do it.' When I ask Kai what pleasure he finds in the challenge he says, 'I just focus on achieving my goal.'

In the past, few knew or cared about being the youngest or fastest person to climb a particular mountain, or sail a particular ocean. Today, every adventure is blogged about, and every climb turns into a record-setting challenge. The more adventurous the record, the more interest it generates. This gives Kai a dilemma. We may complain that achievement too often replaces enjoyment during such challenges, but if Kai wants to inspire others, he has got to play the media game. This means blogging, sitting for photo shoots and giving interviews. He has got to offer something truly spectacular. Like climbing Everest. 'And in fact,' Ed says. 'If Kai decides next week that he's had enough of mountain climbing and wants to swim instead, we'll forget about this whole project and go to the pool.'

31 In the first paragraph, we learn that Kai's aim is

    A to persuade teenagers to exercise more.
    B to become a very well-known person.
    C to encourage teenagers to join him on his expedition.
    D to give people a better impression of teenagers.

32 What does 'it' refer to in line 12 ?

    A climbing five of the Seven Summits
    B being the youngest person to climb Everest
    C climbing Mount Everest and Koscuiszko
    D completing the Seven Summits climbs

33 The experienced climbers that the writer spoke to think that

    A mountain climbing is an unsuitable activity for some teenagers.
    B mountain climbing can help teenagers to develop emotionally.
    C teenagers lack the climbing experience needed to make certain decisions.
    D teenagers are not physically strong enough for mountain climbing.

34 What do we find out about Ed in the third paragraph?

    A He has difficulty dealing with the criticism of others.
    B He wonders whether Kai needs more climbing experience.
    C He has considered the dangers involved in the expedition.
    D He is worried about running out of time to prepare.

35 What is suggested in the fourth paragraph?

    A Ed will use the expedition to find fame.
    B Kai is genuinely interested in climbing Everest.
    C The family should leave the expedition until Kai is older.
    D There is little communication between Kai and his parents.

36 What is the writer's attitude towards Kai in the fifth paragraph?

    A He recognises that Kai needs to do something that attracts attention.
    B He criticises the fact that Kai is only interested in breaking records.
    C He thinks Kai is unwilling to work with the media.
    D He believes Kai should do something even more challenging.

Part 6

You are going to read an article about the invention of roller coasters. Six sentences have been removed from the article. Choose from the sentences **A–G** the one which fits each gap (**37–42**). There is one extra sentence which you do not need to use.

Mark your answers **on the separate answer sheet**.

The history of roller coasters

Roller coasters have a long history, and although most of them are now found in the USA, their origins lie elsewhere.

As early as the 15th century, a popular pastime for Russians was sliding down snow-covered hills on a sledge, much as children still do during the winter in many countries today. **37** These consisted of a wooden slope covered in ice, on top of a wooden frame. Riders sat on large blocks of ice, and the slides, which could be up to 24 metres high, became so popular that even the royal family were said to be fans.

Soldiers returning to France from Russia are thought to have taken with them stories of the 'Russian mountains', and variations of the Russian slides began to appear in France. To make up for the lack of snow and ice, the slides had wooden tracks along which people rode in small cars with wheels. **38** Such freedom of movement meant that they often bumped into each other.

This all changed in 1817, with the opening, in Paris, of two new slides or 'roller coasters', which had cars that were secured to the tracks. Thanks to this improvement, they were now much safer to ride in, which, in turn, meant that they could go faster. **39** However, in 1826 a mechanical system was introduced to drag them up to the start of the ride again.

The following year, a mining company in the USA constructed a railway in Pennsylvania to carry coal in similar small cars from the mine, which was situated at the top of a mountain, to the canal at the bottom.

From there, it could be put on boats. **40** The return trip, however, involved a team of donkeys pulling the cars back up, and took six times as long. In order to solve this problem, a second track was built so that steam engines could be used to do this.

In 1872, with the mine now closed, the railway became a tourist attraction. Visitors came from miles around to travel to the top of the mountain, enjoy the views, and then take the railway down again. **41**

One of the passengers on the railway, Marcus Thompson, saw the potential of such an experience, and decided to construct what we now recognise as the first roller coaster. It opened in 1884 at Coney Island in New York, and was an instant success. Thompson charged 5 cents a ride, and earned his entire investment back in just a few days, such was the popularity of this new ride. By the end of the century, roller coasters could be found at funfairs across the country. **42** It is a battle that continues to this day.

60

A This was built the opposite way around, so that the cars were initially pulled to the top of the slope and then dropped down very suddenly.

B Initially, people had to be employed for the tough job of pushing them back to the top.

C These were not locked in place as they are today, so they tended to slip in all directions as they went down.

D It was this last part of the ride that was memorable as the cars travelled at great speed and round several tight corners.

E Within two hundred years, man-made versions were common in the flatter areas of the country.

F As more and more were built, the need to attract customers meant that manufacturers began to compete to create ever more exhilarating rides.

G The journey involved transporting the load down a steep hill for 14 kilometres and could be completed in only 30 minutes.

Part 7

You are going to read a magazine article in which four teenagers talk about their experiences of taking part in a reality TV series, which aims to find the best young business person. For questions **43–52**, choose from the people (**A–D**). The people may be chosen more than once.

Mark your answers **on the separate answer sheet**.

Which person

learnt that academic ability is not necessary for doing well in business?	43
says they have a competitive nature?	44
was determined to enjoy their experience on the show?	45
discovered that winning the show was not as easy as they had thought?	46
believes you should go into business with people who have similar ambitions?	47
thinks you need a variety of skills to succeed in business?	48
says that if you want success you have to work hard?	49
wanted to change the image of a certain group of people?	50
says the show taught them to appreciate different styles of working?	51
says you should not listen to those who doubt you?	52

Young business people

A — Zoe, 17 years old

I applied to do it because I wanted to show off my talent for business and maybe persuade someone to hire me. I'm a keen viewer of the show, and I'd always wanted to appear on it as I felt I'd be a very strong candidate. I'm the kind of person who won't be beaten, so I felt that the show would be an ideal environment for me. It was exhausting, but also rewarding and fun. I enjoyed all the tasks we had to do. Having had this experience, my advice to other young business people would be: know what you want to do, be creative and decisive and you'll fulfil your potential. Personally, I've learnt that there are all kinds of people in business; it's important to be tolerant of the various ways that people do things, and to value each individual, because everyone has something to offer.

B — Kirsty, 16 years old

As I'm a big fan of the show, it was great to have the opportunity to appear on it. I thought it would be a brilliant way to see how far I could go in the competition and get a taste of working in business. I had the time of my life – it's the best thing I've ever done! I think the experience has made me more confident in my strengths. I'm not that good at some of the stuff we study at school, but I realise now that, with enough determination, I can get to where I want to be in this environment. To anyone hoping to get into business at a young age, stay focused on your goals, and don't be put off by constantly being told what you can't achieve. I've learnt that you have to co-operate in business, and that the work of a team is always more successful than that of an individual.

C — Tim, 18 years old

When the opportunity came up to take part in the show, I just couldn't turn it down. I've always been a fan. Like everyone who watches at home, I always believed I could outdo everyone else – until I was actually there and found out what was expected of me! I loved every minute though. It really made me grow up. I've learned that in the business world a broad range of abilities is necessary to really get on; it's not enough to be very good in just one area. I advise young business people to make sure they put enough effort in if they are to achieve their goals. Natural ability is important of course, but it's not enough on its own.

D — Arjun, 17 years old

I applied for the show because I thought it would give me the opportunity to demonstrate that academics don't just sit and study books all day. Also, I thought it would allow me to learn more about business. I knew that I'd never have the chance to do something like that again so I decided to make the most of every second. Obviously, winning was fantastic, but I think that meeting all those different people during the competition was the real highlight for me. To young businessmen and women, I'd say: never give up on your dreams. If you believe in yourself then anything is possible. From taking part in this show, I've learnt it's vital to join forces with others who share your objectives and that the success of a business depends on the team that's running it and their passion towards whatever it is that's being sold.

WRITING (1 hour 20 minutes)

Part 1

You must answer this question. Write your answer in **140–190** words in an appropriate style.

1 In your English class you have been talking about playing computer games. Now your English teacher has asked you to write an essay for homework.

Write your essay using **all** the notes and giving reasons for your point of view.

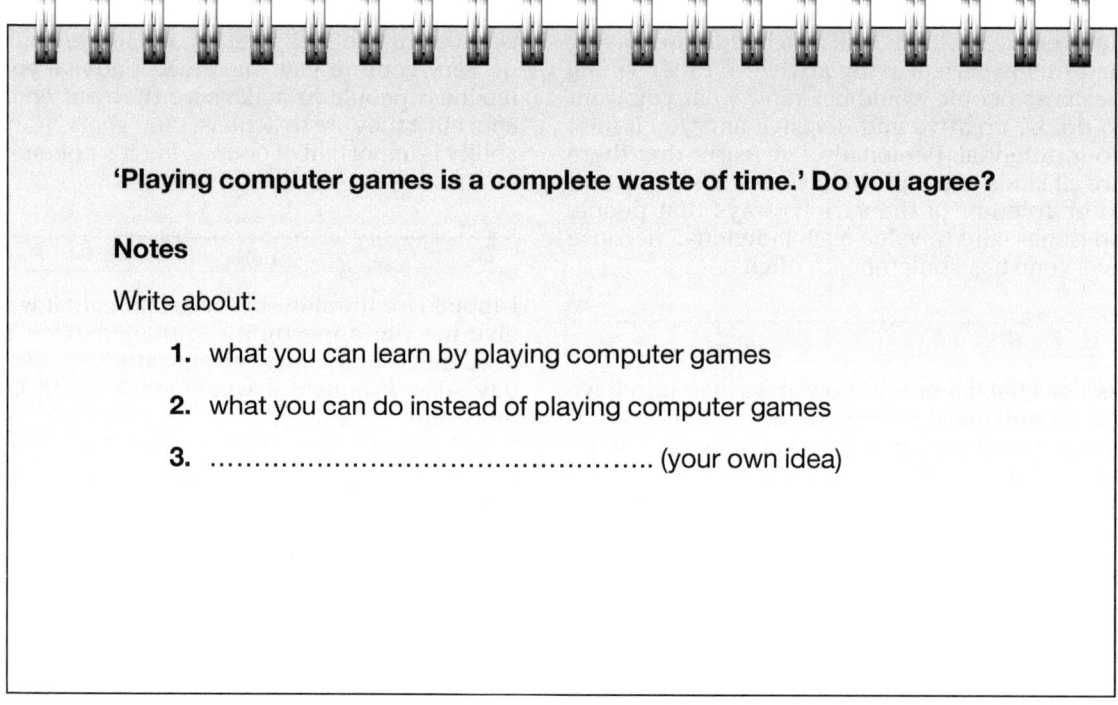

'Playing computer games is a complete waste of time.' Do you agree?

Notes

Write about:

1. what you can learn by playing computer games
2. what you can do instead of playing computer games
3. ……………………………………….. (your own idea)

Part 2

Write an answer to one of the questions **2–5** in this part. Write your answer in **140–190** words in an appropriate style **on the separate answer sheet**. Put the question number in the box at the top of the answer sheet.

---

2   You see this announcement in an English-language magazine for teenagers.

> **Articles wanted**
> ## What makes a perfect school?
> Write an article telling us what **you** think. Write about the teachers, the lessons, the building and anything else you think is important.
>
> We will publish the best articles in next month's magazine.

Write your **article**.

3   You recently saw this notice on an English-language website called *Teen Fun*.

> **Reviews wanted**
> ## A Great Place to Go
> We're looking for reviews of places that young people enjoy going to. It could be a theme park, a leisure centre, a club or somewhere else.
>
> Tell us about a place you go to, what you can do there, and what you like most about it.
>
> The best reviews will be put on our website next month.

Write your **review**.

4   You have seen this announcement in an international magazine for teenagers.

> **Stories wanted**
> We are looking for stories for our new English-language magazine for teenagers. Your story must **begin** with this sentence: *Robert was excited as he jumped into the boat.*
>
> Your story must include:
> - an escape
> - a cave

Write your **story**.

5   Answer the following question based on the title below.

Touching the Void by Joe Simpson

You see this announcement in your school English magazine:

> **Articles wanted**
> We are looking for articles about friendship in the book *Touching the Void*.
> How important is friendship in the story?
> How does the friendship between Joe and Simon change?

Write your **article**.

Test 3

LISTENING (approximately 40 minutes)

Part 1

You will hear people talking in eight different situations. For questions **1–8**, choose the best answer (**A**, **B** or **C**).

1   You hear a girl who is going to live in another country talking to a friend.
    They agree that it will be

    A   exciting to live in a new place.

    B   easy to make new friends.

    C   simple to keep in touch.

2   You hear part of a science programme about a planned space mission to the moons of Jupiter.
    Why does the presenter regard them as a good place to explore?

    A   Something could be living there.

    B   There's a lot of volcanic activity there.

    C   It will show how far it's possible to travel.

3   You hear a girl telling her father about a writer who visited her school.
    What did she think about the writer?

    A   She was pleased to meet him because she enjoys his books.

    B   She was surprised to find out how many books he's written.

    C   She was interested to learn about what inspires him.

4   You hear part of an interview with a girl who is talking about some wolves she saw.
    How did the girl feel when she saw the second wolf?

    A   less afraid than she would have expected

    B   sorry that she was unable to photograph it

    C   grateful that she lives in such an exciting place

5 You hear a young racing driver talking on the radio.
What is the speaker's main purpose?

    A to outline the advantages and disadvantages of his sport

    B to explain what it takes to be a successful racing driver

    C to inform listeners about his own background in racing

6 You overhear a boy talking about a football competition he has been in.
How does he feel?

    A exhausted because of the pressure

    B enthusiastic at getting so far

    C upset because his team didn't win

7 You overhear a girl talking about a club she has recently started going to.
What does she say about it?

    A It's not what she expected.

    B She doesn't enjoy everything about it.

    C She has learnt a lot since joining.

8 You hear a teacher talking to her class about some homework they did.
What do the class need to do better in future assignments?

    A organise their work clearly

    B label visuals appropriately

    C check their work carefully

Test 3

Part 2

You will hear a student called Emily giving a class presentation about a whale watching trip she went on with her family. For questions **9–18**, complete the sentences with a word or short phrase.

Whale watching

The guide on Emily's trip spends most of his time working as a _____ **9**.

At first, Emily found it difficult to tell the difference between a _____ **10** and a whale.

Emily says that the guides used a _____ **11** to communicate with each other.

The fact that many whales have no _____ **12** was one thing that surprised Emily.

It's possible to find out the age of a whale by looking at something inside its _____ **13**.

Emily thought that the _____ **14** of the first whale she saw was an unusual colour.

Emily says that the large whale she saw was similar to a _____ **15** in shape.

To protect the whales, boats have to stay more than _____ **16** metres away from them.

Emily advises anyone who goes whale watching to take a _____ **17** with them.

Emily and her family were lucky enough to see _____ **18** near to the coast.

Part 3

You will hear five short extracts in which teenagers are talking about a new video game. For questions **19–23**, choose from the list (**A–H**) the opinion each speaker expresses. Use the letters only once. There are three extra letters which you do not need to use.

A   It's less exciting than a previous version of the same game.

B   The special effects were what made me interested in it.

Speaker 1	19

C   The pace of it is rather slow.

Speaker 2	20

D   It gives players some interesting choices to make.

Speaker 3	21

E   At first, it's difficult to understand what you have to do.

Speaker 4	22

F   It's likely to appeal to a different age group.

Speaker 5	23

G   The later levels introduce some unusual elements.

H   My friend's better at it than I am.

Test 3

Part 4

You will hear an interview with Jack Herbert, a talented young pianist. For questions **24–30**, choose the best answer (**A**, **B** or **C**).

24 When Jack was a child, his grandmother

    A gave him his first lessons on the piano.

    B sometimes disagreed with his piano teacher.

    C helped him when he found learning the piano difficult.

25 What does Jack say about other members of his family?

    A His brother no longer performs in public.

    B His parents have both played professionally.

    C His sister makes her living as a musician.

26 How did Jack feel during his time at the National Music School?

    A pleased to have the opportunity to be there

    B worried that he wouldn't live up to expectations

    C frustrated that he couldn't choose which pieces to play

27 What is Jack's attitude to practising?

    A He doesn't take it as seriously as he used to.

    B He feels it's essential for good performance.

    C He wishes he didn't have to do so much of it.

28 When he's performing in a live concert, Jack aims to

    A interpret the music in his own way.

    B share his enjoyment of the music with others.

    C play the music better than he's ever done before.

29 Jack thinks that he's different to other pianists of his age because

   A he plays a wider range of musical styles.

   B he brings classical music up to date.

   C he appeals to a young audience.

30 What does Jack plan to do in the future?

   A travel more widely

   B compose more of his own music

   C enter big music competitions

SPEAKING (14 minutes)

You take the Speaking test with another candidate (possibly two candidates), referred to here as your partner. There are two examiners. One will speak to you and your partner and the other will be listening. Both examiners will award marks.

Part 1 (2 minutes)

The examiner asks you and your partner questions about yourselves. You may be asked about things like 'your home town', 'your interests', 'your career plans', etc.

Part 2 (a one-minute 'long turn' for each candidate, plus a 20-second response from the second candidate)

The examiner gives you two photographs and asks you to talk about them for one minute. The examiner then asks your partner a question about your photographs and your partner responds briefly.

Then the examiner gives your partner two different photographs. Your partner talks about these photographs for one minute. This time the examiner asks you a question about your partner's photographs and you respond briefly.

Part 3 (4 minutes)

The examiner asks you and your partner to talk together. You may be asked to solve a problem or try to come to a decision about something. For example, you might be asked to decide the best way to use some rooms in a language school. The examiner gives you some text to help you but does not join in the conversation.

Part 4 (4 minutes)

The examiner asks some further questions, which leads to a more general discussion of what you have talked about in Part 3. You may comment on your partner's answers if you wish.

Test 4

Test 4

READING AND USE OF ENGLISH (1 hour 15 minutes)

Part 1

For questions **1–8**, read the text below and decide which answer (**A**, **B**, **C** or **D**) best fits each gap. There is an example at the beginning (**0**).

Mark your answers **on the separate answer sheet**.

Example:

0   **A** getting   **B** coming   **C** setting   **D** putting

0	A	B	C	D
	■	▢	▢	▢

Cycling holidays

Some of my best holidays have involved **(0)** .... around on two wheels, cycling through the countryside with my family. Our **(1)** .... is for off-road trails where there is no need to worry about other traffic and we can **(2)** .... our time, cycling at our own speed and **(3)** .... for a while to have a rest and **(4)** .... the view. The best routes are away from the crowds but within easy **(5)** .... of accommodation and eating places. Cycling holidays take little planning; we just pick a route, pack essential clothing and set off. Because we have to carry everything with us all the time, we are very strict about what we take – so that **(6)** .... nothing heavy. If you fancy **(7)** .... this a try yourself, there are lots of books and websites that will help you plan a route. There are even companies that will **(8)** .... you with all the equipment you need. So get on your bike and start exploring!

Reading and Use of English

1	**A**	preference	**B**	alternative	**C**	favourite	**D**	option
2	**A**	make	**B**	take	**C**	leave	**D**	catch
3	**A**	waiting	**B**	hesitating	**C**	delaying	**D**	pausing
4	**A**	admire	**B**	regard	**C**	grasp	**D**	observe
5	**A**	distance	**B**	reach	**C**	length	**D**	range
6	**A**	causes	**B**	results	**C**	means	**D**	leads
7	**A**	doing	**B**	making	**C**	having	**D**	giving
8	**A**	offer	**B**	lend	**C**	provide	**D**	recommend

Part 2

For questions **9–16**, read the text below and think of the word which best fits each gap. Use only **one** word in each gap. There is an example at the beginning (**0**).

Write your answers **IN CAPITAL LETTERS on the separate answer sheet**.

Example: | 0 | W | H | A | T | | | | | | | | | | |

Food in space

Have you ever wondered **(0)** .... astronauts eat while they're in space? Well, currently there's not a great deal of choice because making space food is far more difficult than anyone **(9)** .... imagine. The food absolutely **(10)** .... to be nutritious because astronauts' bodies are put under a lot of pressure. They need food in **(11)** .... to maintain their energy levels and keep their spirits up. So scientists are looking for volunteers to help them work **(12)** ....how to improve the quality and choice of food for future space missions. The volunteers will experience exactly what life is **(13)** .... for real astronauts by living inside a fake space capsule and wearing spacesuits. They will spend 120 days living on nothing **(14)** .... space food, recording **(15)** .... time it takes to prepare it, **(16)** .... good it tastes and whether their food choices change over time. At the end of the project, the scientists hope to come up with exciting new food solutions for the astronauts of the future.

Part 3

For questions **17–24**, read the text below. Use the word given in capitals at the end of some of the lines to form a word that fits in the gap **in the same line**. There is an example at the beginning (**0**).

Write your answers **IN CAPITAL LETTERS on the separate answer sheet**.

Example: | 0 | V | I | L | L | A | G | E | R | S | | | | | |

Ancient writing

In 1999, **(0)** ……… in the state of Velacruz, in Mexico, uncovered a stone   **VILLAGE**
block with marks carved onto its surface. **(17)** ……… archaeologists   **MEXICO**
realised how important the marks were: the patterns covering the stone
seemed to provide **(18)** ……… of a system of writing based on pictures   **EVIDENT**
and symbols. The find was particularly **(19)** ……… because it was the   **EXCITE**
oldest example of writing ever found in the region.

The **(20)** ……… patterns, or 'hieroglyphics', include fascinating images   **REMARK**
of snakes and birds. Most experts are aware of the **(21)** ……… of the   **SIGNIFICANT**
find, but there is still some **(22)** ……… about who wrote the ancient   **AGREE**
message. It is hoped that other similar **(23)** ……… in the future will   **DISCOVER**
give researchers a greater degree of certainty about the origins of the
symbols. Experts **(24)** ……… believe they were written by a civilisation   **GENERAL**
known as the Olmecs.

Part 4

For questions **25–30**, complete the second sentence so that it has a similar meaning to the first sentence, using the word given. **Do not change the word given.** You must use between **two** and **five** words, including the word given. Here is an example (**0**).

Example:

0   Prizes are given out when the school year finishes.

   PLACE

   Prize-giving .... end of each school year.

The gap can be filled by the words 'takes place at the', so you write:

Example: | **0** | *TAKES PLACE AT THE*

Write **only** the missing words **IN CAPITAL LETTERS** on the separate answer sheet.

---

25   Wear some warm clothes because it might get cold later.

   CASE

   Wear some warm clothes .... cold later.

26   I really regret eating all that chocolate.

   WISH

   I really .... all that chocolate.

27   'I'm sorry I didn't do my homework,' said Maria.

   NOT

   Maria apologised .... her homework.

28   I missed the train because I got to the station late.

   CAUGHT

   If I had got to the station on time, ... the train.

29 Unfortunately, I only realised I'd lost my keys when I arrived home.

UNTIL

Unfortunately, ………………………………… I arrived home that I realised I'd lost my keys.

30 I'm sure Simon went home early because I can't see him anywhere.

MUST

Simon ………………………………….. home early because I can't see him anywhere.

Part 5

You are going to read a magazine article in which a teenager discusses classical music. For questions **31–36**, choose the answer (**A**, **B**, **C** or **D**) which you think fits best according to the text.

Mark your answers **on the separate answer sheet**.

Teenagers and Classical Music

When you see a teenager with an MP3 player, you can be pretty certain it's not classical music they're listening to. Most of us can list the names of dozens of pop groups, but ask any of my friends if they know who Brahms was and you can tell by the expression on their face that they haven't a clue. I have just started doing a music degree, but the people on my course know no more about the works of great composers than anyone else our age. And if you don't know who wrote the music, you are unlikely to go out and buy any recordings of their work.

The statistics must be depressing for a lover of classical music. Apparently only 3% of concert tickets sold last year were for classical music events, and the average classical recording sells a mere 300 copies. I must say I still find that hard to believe. So what has caused this decline in interest for a type of music that has lasted for centuries? The older generation are irritated by our obsession with TV and video games, blaming it for most things, but I don't think there is any connection in this case. The simple truth is that classical music just doesn't hold much attraction for most people, and that is particularly true of teenagers, who are the ones most likely to buy music and concert tickets.

Now I'm aware that this doesn't apply to everyone my age. I know some teenagers who go to classical music concerts all the time, but they are a minority. Although I am a musician and play in an orchestra, I'm not exactly a classical music fan. I enjoy a huge range of styles, but judging by what's stored on my computer, my classical music consumption is probably pretty close to that 3% figure.

line 34

So why don't teenagers like classical music? Well, first of all, the pace and rhythm of classical music, with its numerous changes of mood, are problematic for us. We like to talk fast, play fast, and think fast. In addition, if you believe the experts, we have difficulty paying attention for more than about three minutes; far too short for most pieces of classical music, but perfect for a pop song. Pop is structurally quite simple and therefore easy to listen to, while appreciating a piece of classical music requires time and concentration. The subject matter of pop music also holds much more appeal than a lengthy piece of classical music with no lyrics. Classical music is incredibly powerful, but not exactly full of the issues that concern teenagers.

The way we listen to music has also changed. In the past, families would gather at home to make music together, and an ability to play an instrument was highly valued. The only other opportunity to hear music was at a concert. Nowadays, you can find any music you want at the click of a mouse, and yet the sound track to our lives is rarely classical. When did you last go into a shop that had classical music playing in the background?

In my orchestra we play classical music in all sorts of different places, but no matter how cool the posters are, I see virtually nothing but grey hair when I look into the crowd. Some say that the lack of interest in classical music among teenagers is the fault of our schools, but there are plenty of kids eager to play classical music in their school orchestra. They arrive early to practise and stay after school to rehearse. Classical music appeals to them when they perform, but otherwise it is not their music of choice. The two activities have become separated. When we want to relax, it's always pop music.

Reading and Use of English

31 In the first paragraph, what does the writer say about teenagers?

  A Their knowledge of classical music is limited to the names of composers.
  B They don't listen to classical music because they don't know what to buy.
  C Even the ones who study music have limited knowledge of classical music.
  D Some would be embarrassed to admit to having classical music on their MP3 player.

32 How does the writer feel about the statistics she mentions in the second paragraph?

  A disappointed that people are losing interest in classical music
  B annoyed that older people criticise the things that she enjoys
  C surprised that so few people buy classical music recordings
  D certain that the future of classical music depends on teenagers

33 What is the meaning of 'classical music consumption' in line 34?

  A the amount of music she listens to
  B the amount of music she plays
  C the number of concerts she attends
  D the number of recordings she has made

34 The writer believes that teenagers prefer pop music because

  A the style of it is always changing.
  B the words used in it are relevant to their lives.
  C it suits their many changes of mood.
  D listening to it helps them to focus.

35 In the fifth paragraph, what does the writer say about classical music?

  A We only really enjoyed it at concerts.
  B We don't notice it being played.
  C We should appreciate the way it is played.
  D We hear it less than other kinds of music.

36 What is the writer's main point in the last paragraph?

  A Pop music is generally more relaxing to listen to than classical music.
  B Those who play classical music often don't like listening to it.
  C Good classical musicians usually have to spend a lot of time practising.
  D Schools are to blame if teenagers are not interested in classical music.

Part 6

You are going to read an article about Antarctica. Six sentences have been removed from the article. Choose from the sentences **A–G** the one which fits each gap (**37–42**). There is one extra sentence which you do not need to use.

Mark your answers **on the separate answer sheet**.

Rainforest in Antarctica

Scientists have discovered that Antarctica looked very different 55 million years ago!

Antarctica is the fifth largest continent after Asia, Africa, North America and South America. It covers 14 million km², 98% of which is ice.

Antarctica is frozen now, but a study has found that there were trees similar to palm trees in the Antarctic 55 million years ago, in a period known as the early Eocene era. **37** Global levels of the principal greenhouse gas, carbon dioxide, were nearly three times as high then as today.

Scientists have known for a long time that the start of the Eocene era was one of the hottest periods in Earth's history, so at that time Antarctica would have been ice free and much warmer than at present. **38**

For millions of years, rock, plants and animal bones have been ground down by wind, water and the sheer weight of ice to tiny pieces known as sediment. Scientists have now analysed samples of Antarctic sediment from the Eocene period. These were not available to them until very recently. **39** Unfortunately, any sediment remaining there from the Eocene period was destroyed as Antarctica's climate changed or buried under thousands of metres of ice.

Now technology has allowed researchers to analyse sediment from under the sea. The study was carried out by a team of 36 scientists off the coast of Antarctica. They dropped a drilling machine through 4 km of water, and used it to make a long thin hole, 1 km deep, into the ocean floor. Then a metal tube was pushed down into the sediment to take a sample, and a sort of lid was closed over it. **40** One of the authors of the study said: 'The samples are the first detailed evidence we have of what was happening in the Antarctic during this vitally important era.'

Throughout the Eocene period, tiny pieces of plant were transported by insects, or washed to the bottom of the sea bed just off the coast. They then settled into the sediment and were preserved for 50 million years. **41** Analysis of the plant pieces in the sediment samples reveals that the coast of Antarctica used to be covered in warm rainforest similar to that in northern Australia or New Guinea. Further inland, mountainous regions were covered in different kinds of trees.

This discovery suggests that temperatures on the Antarctic coast were around 16°C and summers reached a pleasant 21°C. Antarctica was in nearly the same position as it is now, over the South Pole. As a result, it would have been dark in winter, like today. **42** Temperatures probably never fell below 10°C.

The vegetation of Antarctica is very different today from 55 million years ago. There are no trees or bushes on the continent, and only two species of flowering plants are found along the western side of the Antarctic Peninsula. What will it be like, though, in another 50 million years?

A The main reason for this is that they had previously only been able to look on land.

B So they decided to collect some more samples in winter, despite the difficulties involved.

C The presence of particular plants, however, indicates that it was fairly warm even during those coldest months.

D They could grow there because at that time the area had a near-tropical climate with frost-free winters, even in the polar darkness.

E Some of them have now been brought up in the tubes.

F But their new findings have provided the first ever detailed information about its environment and, consequently, its climate.

G This ensured it remained inside as it was pulled out.

Test 4

Part 7

You are going to read an article in which four teenage girls describe school trips they have been on. For questions **43–52**, choose from the people (**A–D**). The people may be chosen more than once.

Mark your answers **on the separate answer sheet**.

Which person

recommends something she did?	43
appreciates having made new friends?	44
regretted a choice she made?	45
was persuaded to do something which proved enjoyable?	46
thought of ideas for group activities?	47
had concerns that were shared by other people?	48
was reassured by a good first impression?	49
is not sure she was told the truth?	50
enjoyed some activities more than other people did?	51
had expected some people to behave differently?	52

School trips

A Lisa

The trip was organised at the beginning of the academic year because we hadn't seen each other much over the summer. It was basically six days doing activities like mountain walking and canoeing. We offered to help with the cooking, which was actually quite good fun. The plan was that we would do things all together in the evenings; my friends and I came up with stuff like games and talent shows, and we even put on a play one night. We performed it for the teachers, who really liked it – at least, that's what they said at the time! It didn't really matter anyway, because we all had such a laugh. Some friends of mine even posted a video of it online when we got home. I hope we can do something like that again some time.

B Rosa

I must admit I expected it to be a bit of a waste of time. This trip was compulsory for the whole class, and I thought it might be dreadful! Anyway, when we got off the train and I saw the lovely village where we were staying, I knew straight away it would be all right. Our teachers were really friendly and did loads of sports with us, which was perfect for me, but not that great for some of my less sporty friends. On one day we could choose to go either to a museum or to an art gallery. I went to the museum, which was a poor decision as the alternative, the art gallery, was pretty cool and everyone should see it apparently. All in all, though, I had a great time and I'll definitely be on the next trip!

C Claire

We were away for three days, and on one of them we visited a huge cave. I was anxious about going underground into the dark! All my friends teased me about that but said I'd be OK and that they'd look after me, so I went along. I didn't like it at all at first, but when I eventually relaxed and started to look around properly, I have to say it was stunning. There were lights along all the paths inside the cave and they'd also put some up so you could see the different rock formations there. So in the end, it wasn't scary at all. The rest of the trip was fun too, but I'd say that was the highlight. I wish I could go back there with my family, but it's too far away. But should you be in that area, it is definitely worth a visit.

D Jana

I hadn't wanted to go on any school trips before because I was worried about being away from my parents. I know it sounds silly, but I also know I wasn't the only one. There was no choice this time; the whole class had to go. It was only for the weekend in any case, and not far from home either. We went camping – luckily, it didn't rain. I thought the teachers might be strict with us, but that wasn't the case at all. We went for long walks in the forest during the day, but probably the best bit was in the evenings when we sat round a campfire in a big circle and sang funny songs. I even ended up getting close to people I'd never talked to much at school before, so the trip really was worthwhile.

WRITING (1 hour 20 minutes)

Part 1

You must answer this question. Write your answer in **140–190** words in an appropriate style.

1. In your English class you have been talking about playing different sports. Now your English teacher has asked you to write an essay for homework.

   Write your essay using **all** the notes and giving reasons for your point of view.

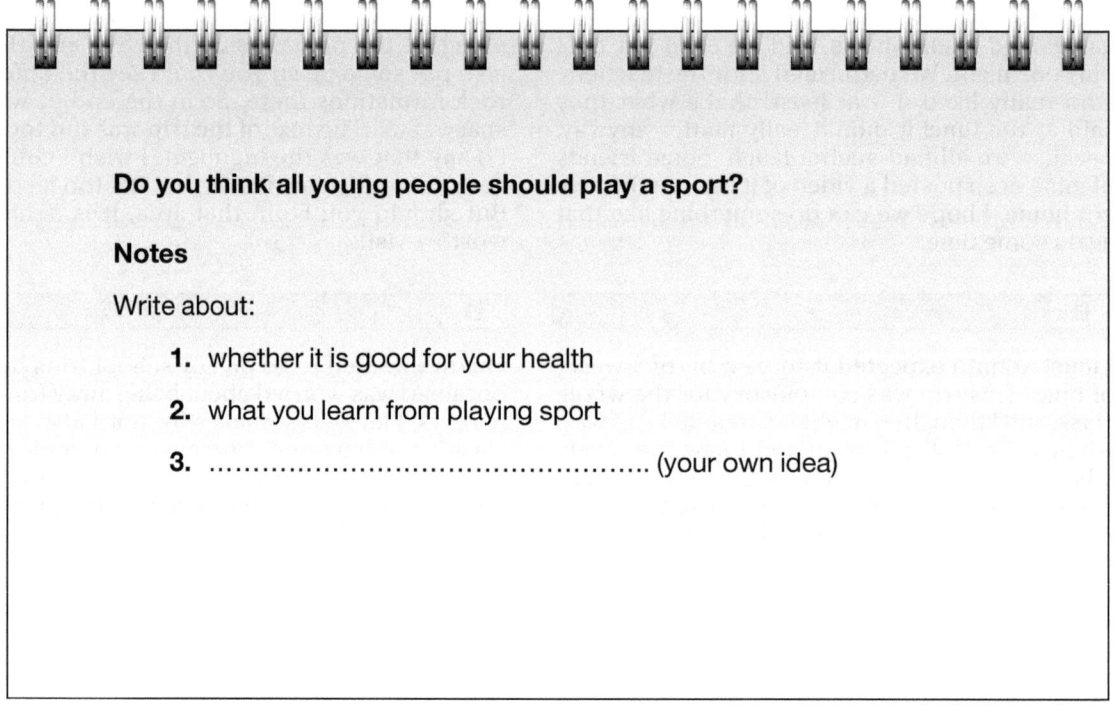

Do you think all young people should play a sport?

Notes

Write about:

1. whether it is good for your health
2. what you learn from playing sport
3. ………………………………………….. (your own idea)

Part 2

Write an answer to one of the questions **2–5** in this part. Write your answer in **140–190** words in an appropriate style **on the separate answer sheet**. Put the question number in the box at the top of the answer sheet.

2   You have just received this letter from your Canadian friend, Sam.

> As you know, I've just moved to another town and I'm starting at my new school next week. I'm really excited but I don't know anybody yet. What should I do to make friends at school? And how could I meet people near where I live?
>
> Write and tell me what you think.
>
> Sam

Write your **letter**.

3   You recently saw this notice on an international film website for teenagers.

> **Reviews wanted**
>
> ### A film all teenagers should see
>
> Which film would you recommend to young people of your age? Write a review telling us about the story and the main characters, and explain why you think it is a good film for teenagers to see.
>
> The best reviews will be put on our website.

Write your **review**.

4   You have seen this announcement in a new English-language magazine for schools:

> **Stories wanted**
>
> We are looking for stories for our new English-language magazine for teenagers. Your story must begin with this sentence:
>
> *I got to the station and waited nervously for the train to arrive.*
>
> Your story must include:
> - a meeting
> - a photograph

Write your **story**.

5   Answer the following question based on the title below.

Macbeth by William Shakespeare

Your English class has had a discussion about the characters in the story of Macbeth. Now your teacher has given you this essay for homework:

Why are the three witches important in the story of Macbeth?

Write your **essay**.

Test 4

LISTENING (approximately 40 minutes)

Part 1

You will hear people talking in eight different situations. For questions **1–8**, choose the best answer (**A**, **B** or **C**).

1   You overhear two friends talking about a lesson they had at school.
    What surprised them in the lesson?

    A how astronomers are able to research distant stars

    B the reason for the particular location of a star

    C the temperature and size of the sun

2   You hear two friends talking about buying a card game for the boy's sister.
    What is the girl's opinion of it?

    A It doesn't suit his sister's character.

    B It's not appropriate for someone of his sister's age.

    C It's a game that's better for boys than girls.

3   You hear part of an interview on the radio with a writer of children's books.
    The writer thinks that books are more powerful than films because

    A they affect you in a very personal and vivid way.

    B they allow you to share the characters' inner thoughts.

    C they stay in your memory longer than films do.

4   You hear a guide speaking to tourists.
    What is the guide talking about?

    A when different exhibitions are on

    B what's on display in the exhibitions

    C the best way to go round the exhibitions

5 You hear two friends talking about a musical festival they are going to attend.
What is the boy looking forward to most?

  A learning who the surprise performer will be

  B having the chance to see new performers

  C hearing some performers he liked last year

6 You hear two friends talking about a movie.
What do they agree about?

  A The plot was handled appropriately.

  B The visual effects were stunning.

  C The actors were well chosen.

7 You hear two friends talking about a news story about a baby monkey.
What do they agree about?

  A that the monkey is in the best environment for it

  B that the monkey deserves better treatment

  C that it is sad this species of monkey is endangered

8 You overhear two friends talking about their holidays.
How does the boy feel about his holiday?

  A surprised about how much he enjoyed his holiday

  B disappointed that the family's plans had to change

  C pleased that he was able to learn a new skill

Test 4

Part 2

You will hear a student called Shirley Bailey giving a talk at her school about her experience of working at a wildlife centre in Africa last summer. For questions **9–18**, complete the sentences with a word or short phrase.

Greenwood Wildlife Centre

When looking for a place to work, Shirley first asked at a [**9**] near a relative's home.

Shirley explains that Greenwood informs [**10**] about earning extra income from protecting wildlife.

Shirley found dealing with [**11**] was the hardest task she had to do at Greenwood.

Shirley was surprised how much she enjoyed doing [**12**] with certain animals.

Shirley worked on what was called the [**13**] project.

Shirley explains that, generally, animals are put into [**14**] when they are well enough to leave the zoo.

Shirley found that [**15**] was her only regular expense after she had arrived at Greenwood.

Shirley says that the best thing about her accommodation was its location near to the [**16**].

The centre advised volunteers to wear [**17**] while they were working.

Greenwood provided the volunteers with [**18**] to use.

Part 3

You will hear five short extracts in which teenagers are talking about the sports they take part in. For questions **19–23**, choose from the list (**A–H**) what each speaker says about their sport. Use the letters only once. There are three extra letters which you do not need to use.

A   An injury stopped me doing it for a while.

B   I'm going to take a special course to improve my skills.

Speaker 1 [ ] 19

C   I was surprised how much time I needed for it.

Speaker 2 [ ] 20

D   I enjoy competitions more than training.

Speaker 3 [ ] 21

E   It has helped me make a lot of new friends.

Speaker 4 [ ] 22

F   The weather sometimes spoils my enjoyment.

Speaker 5 [ ] 23

G   A member of my family encouraged me to take it up.

H   My club provides all the equipment I need.

Part 4

You will hear part of an interview with Roberto Gianni, a fashion designer. For questions **24–30**, choose the best answer (**A**, **B** or **C**).

---

24 When Roberto was a teenager, he felt he needed

  A to show his friends he was capable of originality.

  B to prove he was better at design than his friends.

  C to help his friends create good-looking clothes.

25 What gave Roberto his big chance to break into the fashion industry?

  A going to college to study design

  B coming up with an award-winning design

  C being interviewed by a fashion magazine

26 How does Roberto feel about the clothes he designs now?

  A He thinks they are more glamorous than his early designs.

  B He's making clothes that match his own personal taste.

  C He believes his designs appeal to different age groups.

27 What does Roberto regard as the biggest influence on his work?

  A other more famous designers

  B fashion shows he's attended

  C the fashions of the past

28 How did Roberto's parents react to his choice of career?

  A They gave him their support.

  B They tried to change his mind.

  C They didn't think he was serious.

29 How does Roberto feel when people are critical of his work?

  A He gets upset that they don't understand what he's trying to do.

  B He remains confident about what he's doing.

  C He is determined to use their feedback constructively.

30 What advice does Roberto have for teenagers who want to become designers?

  A find work to gain experience in the business

  B study fashion seriously and remain open to new ideas

  C create a wide range of designs to show professionals

Test 4

SPEAKING (14 minutes)

You take the Speaking test with another candidate (possibly two candidates), referred to here as your partner. There are two examiners. One will speak to you and your partner and the other will be listening. Both examiners will award marks.

Part 1 (2 minutes)

The examiner asks you and your partner questions about yourselves. You may be asked about things like 'your home town', 'your interests', 'your career plans', etc.

Part 2 (a one-minute 'long turn' for each candidate, plus a 20-second response from the second candidate)

The examiner gives you two photographs and asks you to talk about them for one minute. The examiner then asks your partner a question about your photographs and your partner responds briefly.

Then the examiner gives your partner two different photographs. Your partner talks about these photographs for one minute. This time the examiner asks you a question about your partner's photographs and you respond briefly.

Part 3 (4 minutes)

The examiner asks you and your partner to talk together. You may be asked to solve a problem or try to come to a decision about something. For example, you might be asked to decide the best way to use some rooms in a language school. The examiner gives you some text to help you but does not join in the conversation.

Part 4 (4 minutes)

The examiner asks some further questions, which leads to a more general discussion of what you have talked about in Part 3. You may comment on your partner's answers if you wish.

Sample answer sheet: Reading and Use of English

SAMPLE

Candidate Name
If not already printed, write name in CAPITALS and complete the Candidate No. grid (in pencil).

Candidate Signature

Examination Title

Centre

Supervisor:
If the candidate is ABSENT or has WITHDRAWN shade here ▭

Centre No.

Candidate No.

Examination Details

Candidate Answer Sheet

Instructions

Use a PENCIL (B or HB).

Rub out any answer you wish to change using an eraser.

Parts 1, 5, 6 and 7:
Mark ONE letter for each question.

For example, if you think **B** is the right answer to the question, mark your answer sheet like this:

| 0 | A | B̷ | C | D |

Parts 2, 3 and 4:
Write your answer clearly in CAPITAL LETTERS.

For Parts 2 and 3 write one letter in each box. For example:

| 0 | E | X | A | M | P | L | E |

Part 1

1. A B C D
2. A B C D
3. A B C D
4. A B C D
5. A B C D
6. A B C D
7. A B C D
8. A B C D

Part 2

Do not write below here

9.
10.
11.
12.
13.
14.
15.
16.

Continues over ➡

© UCLES 2014 Photocopiable

Sample answer sheet: Reading and Use of English

Sample answer sheet: Listening

CAMBRIDGE ENGLISH
Language Assessment
Part of the University of Cambridge

SAMPLE

Candidate Name
If not already printed, write name in CAPITALS and complete the Candidate No. grid (in pencil).

Candidate Signature

Examination Title

Centre

Supervisor:
If the candidate is ABSENT or has WITHDRAWN shade here

Centre No.

Candidate No.

Examination Details

Candidate Answer Sheet

Instructions

Use a PENCIL (B or HB).
Rub out any answer you wish to change using an eraser.

Parts 1, 3 and **4:**
Mark ONE letter for each question.

For example, if you think **B** is the right answer to the question, mark your answer sheet like this:

Part 2:
Write your answer clearly in CAPITAL LETTERS.

Write one letter or number in each box.
If the answer has more than one word, leave one box empty between words.

For example:

Turn this sheet over to start.

© UCLES 2014 Photocopiable

Sample answer sheet: Listening

Thanks and acknowledgements

The authors and publishers acknowledge the following sources of copyright material and are grateful for the permissions granted. While every effort has been made, it has not always been possible to identify the sources of all the material used, or to trace all copyright holders. If any omissions are brought to our notice, we will be happy to include the appropriate acknowledgements on reprinting.

Text acknowledgements

Straw Hat for the text on p. 14 adapted from *Queen Rider*. Copyright © Straw Hat Publishers 2014; The Toronto Star for the text on p. 16 adapted from 'Toronto Teens Send Lego Man on a Balloon Odyssey 24 Kilometers High' by Kate Allen, *The Toronto Star*, 25.01.2012. Copyright © 2012 by *The Toronto Star*; Redwings Horse Sanctuary for the text on p. 32 adapted from 'All About Horses...' www.redwings.org.uk. Copyright © The Redwings Horse Sanctuary; Random House Canada for the text on p. 36 adapted from *First Descent* by Pam Withers. Copyright © 2011 by Pam Withers; Dogo News for the text on p. 38 adapted from 'Need Electricity? Play a Game of Soccer!' by Meera Dolasia, 01.08.2012. Copyright © 2012 by Dogo News; text on p. 60 adapted from 'The History of Rollercoasters.' ThrillNetwork.com.

Photo acknowledgements

Key: T = Top, C = Centre, B = Below.

C1(T): Getty Images/© Ramiro Olaciregui; C1(B): Getty Images/© Ariel Skelley; C2(T): Getty Images/© Bob Thomas; C2(B): Corbis/© Andersen Ross/Blend Ross; C4(T): Getty Images/© Tyler Edwards/Digital Vision; C4(B): Getty Images/© Dennis Hallinan; C5(T): Corbis©/Kerrick James; C5(B): Getty Images/© Vicky Kasala/ Digital Vision; C7(T): Getty Images/© LWA; C7(B):Getty Images/ © Peter Dazeley; C8(T): Alamy/© Blend Images; C8(B): Corbis/© Maxie Productions/Blend Images; C10(T): Alamy/© Martyn Williams; C10(B): Alamy/© Alvey & Towers Picture Library; C11(T): Alamy/© David Willis; C11(B): Corbis/© Franz-Marc Frei; p.60 (Test 3, Part 6): Shutterstock/© Tom Hirtreifer.

The recordings which accompany this book were made at dsound, London.